learning
can be child's play

learning can be child's play

How Parents Can Help Slower-Than-Average Preschool Children
Learn and Develop Through Play Experiences

june mather

illustrated by
martha perske

ABINGDON   Nashville

LEARNING CAN BE CHILD'S PLAY

Library of Congress Cataloging in Publication Data

ISBN 0-687-21317-7

Mather, June, 1924-
    Learning can be child's play.

    1. Play. 2. Slow learning children. 3. Mentally handicapped
children—Education. I. Title.
LB1137.M277   371.9'26   76-20610

MANUFACTURED BY THE PARTHENON PRESS AT
NASHVILLE, TENNESSEE, UNITED STATES OF AMERICA

. . . . . to leslie

preface

Children who are not keeping up with their peers in school are given special attention with special teachers and special programs. But there are seldom any experts around the home to give daily advice on what to do when babies or preschool children show signs of lagging behind. This book is written for parents of children like this. It is a how-to book. It is an attempt to show how some of the latest ideas in early childhood development can be used to help babies and preschool children in the home. It uses real-life examples to explain the pleasures and pitfalls encountered in bringing up children who are slower than average.

This book is based on two main themes. The first is the idea of developmental sequence, which is widely accepted nowadays because of the research of Piaget, Bruner, and Gesell. From this comes an understanding of the learning process—that learning comes about step by step, and, to paraphrase Professor Jerome Bruner, that simple activities have to be mastered before more complicated tasks can be attempted. The second theme is that children learn while playing and that everyday routine can be changed into "child's play" or into experiences from which they can learn.

I have written from my experiences as a teacher in an experimental preschool for two- to four-year-old developmentally delayed children. Some of the ideas in the book were originally contained in my booklet *Make the Most of Your Baby*, which was published by the National Association for Retarded Citizens in January 1974 as part of an ongoing public information program made possible by a grant from the Civitan Clubs of North America.

contents

1. a new point of view

Billy and Jeff decided to cover a wall with big sheets of construction paper. They pasted the paper to the wall with cellophane tape. Much of the time the tape became twisted and stuck to itself as they pulled it from the roll. After they had had to throw away several yards of it, I reprimanded the boys, telling them not to be so wasteful.

Doug loved to paint, but he could not resist painting the wall beside him. No matter how often I scolded him and how many times I told him to keep his brush on the paper in front of him, the moment my back was turned, quick as a flash he would paint the wall again.

If I told you the ages or the IQs of the children above, it might excuse their behavior. However, it would not excuse mine. I call myself a teacher, and here are but two examples of my total insensitivity to the needs of my pupils and my lack of understanding of the learning process.

Jeff and Billy—after patiently listening to me—continued their project. During the next few hours they were happily occupied together, creating a colorful wall design. By the time they proudly showed me the finished result, they were beginning to get the hang of working with the cellophane tape. True, most of the roll ended up in the wastepaper basket, but considering that it cost only twenty-seven cents, I figured it was a pretty inexpensive learning experience for them.

It was a pretty inexpensive learning experience for me as well—and a very valuable one—for I discovered that, often, children left to themselves learn a more important lesson than the one I was trying to teach them. In other words, children teach themselves if they are provided with a suitable environment.

What about my painter friend Douglas? His actions spoke so clearly, yet it took so long for me to understand what he was trying to tell me. In his short life, Doug had never come across an artist creating an imaginary world on canvas on an easel in front of him. The only adults he had ever seen with brushes and cans of paint in their hands wore white overalls and hats, built scaffolds, climbed ladders, and painted rooms and whole houses! A big brush, a bucket of water, and a wall that could stand being wet were all that he needed to join, in his imagination, those heroic grown-ups he admired so much.

As for the lesson that Douglas taught me, it was this: in order to mold the life of any child, it is first necessary to see that particular child's world, to look at it through *his* eyes, and to measure it against *his* own past experience.

These are but two of the many things I learned from an exceptional group of children. They were labeled trainable or educable mentally handicapped, and they included those with learning disabilities, brain damage, autism, slow development, epilepsy, cerebral palsy, emotional and behavior problems, and mental retardation.

After many years of being involved with these school-age children, I began teaching slower-than-average two- and three-year-olds. I soon discovered that the same lessons applied to infants as young as this. The more you know them individually and understand their needs, the easier it is to teach them.

This is why parents are so often such good teachers, because they know and understand their child better than anyone else. Parents in fact, and more especially mothers usually, are the *only* teachers children have in those important and formative first few years of life. A mother is often referred to as her baby's first teacher because she guides her newborn child through all the tremendous changes that take place in the early years.

Many mothers do this with no previous experience in bringing up babies. In fact, success does not depend on previous experience, nor does it depend on intelligence or academic background. It is sometimes explained as an instinct, but I believe that a successful mother is one who learns *from her baby* how best to guide him in the early years. Her baby shows her, by his responses, how she can most effectively teach him, just as Jeff and Billy and Douglas showed me by their behavior how I could most effectively teach them.

Problems occur when the responses are slow in

coming. When the baby is not doing as well as other children, parents naturally become worried. They may try to push him beyond his ability, and this can lead to emotional problems. Or they may overprotect him, doing things *for* him rather than encouraging him to do things for himself. This can hinder his progress even more.

Before you can discover how best to help your particular child, there are two simple rules you must have in mind. One rule is, no matter how much slower than average your child may be, *he is first and foremost a child and a human being*. He has needs—the same basic needs as any other human infant. Suitable food, proper clothing, adequate rest, sufficient exercise, a protected environment, and loving attention are as necessary to the slower-than-average as to any other child. The trick is that the simple, everyday routine of eating, dressing, bathing, and playing can be changed into experiences which will help your child's development. All of which leads to the second rule—*you can change day-to-day routine into meaningful learning experiences for your baby*. To do this you do not need special skills, but you do need a new point of view. Everything should be looked at with an eye to its possibility as a teaching aid. In order for you to look at routine things with an eye to their potential teaching value there are a few things you should know about development.

development

When children are described as being slower than average, developmentally delayed, mentally or intellectually retarded, lagging behind, or having learning difficulties or disabilities, a comparison is being made between them and other children of the same age. They are being compared with average children.

Many studies have been made in the last several decades and many books have been written which describe in detail all the things average children are able to do at different ages. Thus we learn, for example, the average baby turns over at x months, sits at y months, walks at z months, and says his first word at m years. This makes for discouraging reading for those whose child did not sit up until he was y plus four or five months and did not say his first word until he was m plus five or ten years or not even then.

However, these lists of achievements are of value, for they show that development is not a haphazard affair. It is a systematic, orderly process. All children go through the same sequence of development. All children go from one stage of development to the next *in the same order*.

The amount of time spent at each stage differs in every child. The rate of development varies. Some children spend a long time at each stage. Some spend longer at one stage than at the next. Others race past some stages so quickly it appears they have actually skipped or missed them completely.

All of us have heard of children like this—children who never crawled, for instance, but one day got up directly from a sitting position and began to walk. I have even come across youngsters who never seemed to babble or make sounds and who suddenly began to talk using words and phrases.

Children like this are the exception rather than the rule. There is no particular advantage in skipping or missing stages of development; in fact, in the case of the slower-than-average it may be quite harmful.

Every stage or step of development is nicely designed to bring into use the sets of muscles which will be needed in the following stages. Thus each stage becomes a preparation for the next. When your baby crawls on the floor he is using and learning to control some of the same muscles he will need when he begins to walk. While he lies on his stomach in his crib and lifts his head to see what he can see, he is using the same neck and back muscles which will eventually help him to stand up. When you introduce your baby to solid food, he will have to exercise control over his tongue and lips, which, later on, will enable him to speak properly. The more proficient he is in one stage of development, the easier it will be for him in the next. Poor posture, awkward

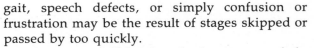

gait, speech defects, or simply confusion or frustration may be the result of stages skipped or passed by too quickly.

It may very well be that the best way to help your baby is to go back to an earlier stage of development and have him get a bit more practice there just for fun. You can make a game out of it perhaps, or turn it into play. When your child is beginning to say words, you will find he gets great enjoyment from going back to earlier stages of speech development and making silly sounds, animal noises, and singing his favorite songs over and over again. Once he has started to walk, it will help him to gain strength if you can occasionally encourage him to creep or crawl again, under the table, over the sofa, or through a tunnel.

This kind of play activity is so much better for progress of the slower-than-average than being pushed beyond his capacity. I once came across a mother who taught her little boy to write the alphabet the moment he was able to handle a pencil. This created quite a problem for Donald, and it showed up one day when he was helping to draw a face on the blackboard. He correctly marked the nose and the mouth and then triumphantly made the letter *i* twice, complete with dots, for eyes! This type of confusion can be avoided if you understand there are no shortcuts in development and that it is better to proceed slowly and surely one step at a time.

It is that very first step that is the important one to watch out for—the very first time your baby holds his head up, for instance. Take note of this event. Now you know that he is *able* to do this. After he has held his head up for the first time for a moment or two, you can then provide him with opportunities to repeat this action. Do this by putting him in a position where he *can* hold his head up—in other words, lay him on his tummy rather than his back. Sometimes stroking his back or placing a small, firm pillow under his arms and beneath his chest will encourage him to hold his head up. An interesting sound to listen to or a bright object to look at will give him a reason to want to hold his head up.

Every day give him the opportunity to practice this new skill. Give him plenty of praise for doing it too, and soon you will see that he is able to hold his head up for longer and longer periods of time as his neck and back muscles become stronger and more controlled.

Follow this same procedure with all tasks and activities. Be on the lookout for "first times" so you can provide opportunities for the second time, the second stage or step, then for the next one and the one that follows that.

You will discover that all skills, tasks, and activities can be broken down into small, simple steps: feeding and dressing, for example. The first step comes when your baby puts his hands on the spoon or bottle, or holds his arms out to "help" you dress him. Watch for these moments and encourage them. Enclose his hand in yours on the bottle or spoon as you feed him. When you pull his hat off, take his hand in yours and remove the hat together. Later on, make a game out of it: pull it down over his eyes and let him reach up and take it off himself!

Encourage your child to do more and more for himself. Think of his learning as something you and he will do together just for fun. Praise him and make sure that he is having fun and enjoying himself with you. Never let him become tired or bored or restless. It is through play that little children learn and develop, so make sure that his learning experiences are playful and pleasant ones.

There are two different aspects of development that must be considered. First, there is each individual child's own schedule of development, which is rather like a train moving from one stage or station to the next—going very slowly and perhaps even stopping at some stages and then rushing past others on the way.

Second, remember that all skills, activities, and tasks you want your child to be able to do can be broken down into small steps that can be accomplished one at a time, each single step needing to be perfected before he reaches for the next one until the whole task, skill, or activity is successfully completed.

Your child's development occurs in both of these ways: first the use and control of his own body, and, second, the performance of tasks, skills, and activities.

Some parents are told right at birth that their baby is going to develop at a slower than average rate. This is particularly true in the case of Down's Syndrome, which is diagnosed primarily by certain physical characteristics. At this early stage it is often very difficult to see any actual evidence of lag in development. Babies are babies, and they all seem to act pretty much alike.

In any event, it is not the difference in development that is important. The important thing to understand is *how* a baby develops, even a retarded one—perhaps especially a retarded one.

Babies cry. Babies cry for a very specific reason. They cry to attract attention. Right here—at this very point—it is time to think about using the cry of a baby to help his development.

The way to do this is to make the baby *wait a moment or two* before you go to him. This is to give the baby *time*—time to realize that the loud sound he hears is his own crying, time to connect that loud sound with the discomfort which caused it.

Such things as wetness, hunger, cold, loneliness, or fright cause discomfort. Naturally a newborn baby has no way of knowing why he is uncomfortable. He just knows he is, and so he cries. His mother hears him. She changes him if he is wet. She feeds him if he is hungry, and she comforts him if he is lonely or frightened. This is what his crying has achieved—it has given him his mother.

Probably this is nature's way of ensuring the survival of the most helpless of all creatures, a newborn human being. It is an elementary method of communication—the way a tiny baby tells his mother: "I am unhappy . . . I need help."

Some mothers worry when their babies cry. Perhaps they are afraid of disturbing neighbors or other members of the family. Perhaps they feel guilty about allowing their babies to experience need or discomfort. In any event, they try to prevent them from crying in the first place, and they do this by anticipating their needs. They feed them before they are hungry, and they change them before they have had a chance to realize they are wet. What happens in these cases is that the babies make less and less effort on their own behalf, less and less demand for attention.

Of course, the opposite is also true. There are mothers who never respond when their babies cry. This can be equally unrewarding, because these babies never learn that their cries of discomfort are ways of calling for their mothers.

Some slower-than-average babies are described as being very content and easy to take care of, and I often wonder if this might be because they have not been given the opportunity to experience *need*. Maybe "contentment" in this case is really lack of effort.

Other retarded babies are described as being very restless and fussy. Is it possible that this could be because these children's early cries for attention went unheeded? These babies never learned that crying is a method of communication.

So, for a start, give your child time to experience need, and time to realize how to attract your attention. On the other hand, do not keep him waiting too long. You are the person who has to decide how long is long enough. You can tell because you are the one who knows your baby best.

When you have given him just the amount of time you think he should have, go to him. Go to him, but do not immediately grab him up out of his crib, pull his wet diapers off, and change him right away, or automatically stick a bottle in his mouth. Again, give him a moment or two—time to become aware of your presence. Smile at him. Talk to him. Hold his hand and try to make him look at you. At first, of course, he will not respond, but in time he will recognize the sound of your voice and his face will light up when he sees you. This is called eye contact.

Making eye contact (ear or hand contact in the case of babies who have severe eye problems) is a more advanced method of communication; it is two-way communication. You have his full attention, and *he has yours*. Crying is a way of signaling unhappiness and asking for help; eye contact welcomes another person and says "Hello, I'm glad to see you" without using words.

Responding to another particular human being is what eye contact is all about. It is a big step from the simple, one-way cry for attention. It is an important and very basic step. It involves the individual's recognition of his dependence upon another person. Just as it takes two to tango, it takes two people to make eye contact.

For many slower-than-average children this step may take a long time—years perhaps. (But the constant repetition of the actions described above will help them to achieve it.) This is because some slower-than-average children have trouble focusing attention for a length of time, while others have difficulty shifting attention from one thing to another.

Johnny belonged to the former group. He was a hyperactive little boy who hardly ever looked at another person because his attention was constantly diverted by other things. He would pick up a ball, but drop it almost at once as his eye was caught by a bright object in the corner of the room; then, as he made his way toward *that,* a movement from outside the window would draw him in yet another direction. He was like a top spinning in a kaleidoscope world. It seemed as if it would be impossible for him to slow down enough to make eye contact, but every so often his eye would catch another person's and his whole face would light up.

Mel had spent his early years in an orphanage. He showed no interest in toys, other children, or adults. As a matter of fact, he took adults completely for granted—they were simply creatures who fed and clothed him and occasionally gave him affection. He accepted their aid with minimal interest. When left to his own devices he would lie on his back on the floor and stare at the ceiling, repeatedly turning his head from side to side until he almost put himself into a kind of trance. He seemed to enjoy doing this so much that he became quite angry when he was made to do something else. But he did make eye contact one day with me, and it all came about unexpectedly.

One day, when I had all but decided that he could not be reached at all, I picked him up and tossed him in the air. He was so delighted with the experience that from that time on he would clamber onto my lap and demand that I do it over and over again. If I pretended I did not understand what he wanted, he not only made eye contact but he told me with his whole body what he wanted from me.

From this chance episode Mel began to see the advantage of responding to another human being. At the same time, I began to see that you never know, until you try it, what will make a child respond to you. But with babies it seems to be different . . .

Have you ever noticed other people when they are looking at a tiny baby? Have you ever wondered what it is about a newborn human being that brings out the clown in all of us? Perhaps it is instinctive to make funny faces and odd sounds to babies. Whatever the reason, we continue to behave this way until the baby reacts to our performance. He smiles, and this is the applause we need—the response we played the jester to produce.

The smiling response is an important milestone for a baby. Now he knows how to signal his delight, how to show his contentment, how to say "I am happy." Smiling, like crying, is the way a tiny baby communicates with us. Unlike crying, which was caused by discomfort, smiling has been caused by us.

Making faces and funny noises is only one way of getting a baby to smile. Every day mothers and fathers find new ways of making their babies respond with delight.

Often a baby's first smile is observed at feeding time and is sometimes, rather scornfully, dismissed as passing wind. A mother is not so easily put off. She knows smiles start not in the mouth, but in the eyes. For a baby, feeding is a great deal more than just food. A human baby has to be held in order to be fed. So feeding is not only warm milk in his mouth, but warm arms cuddling him close to a warm body—and a gentle voice and a familiar face all encouraging him to smile in

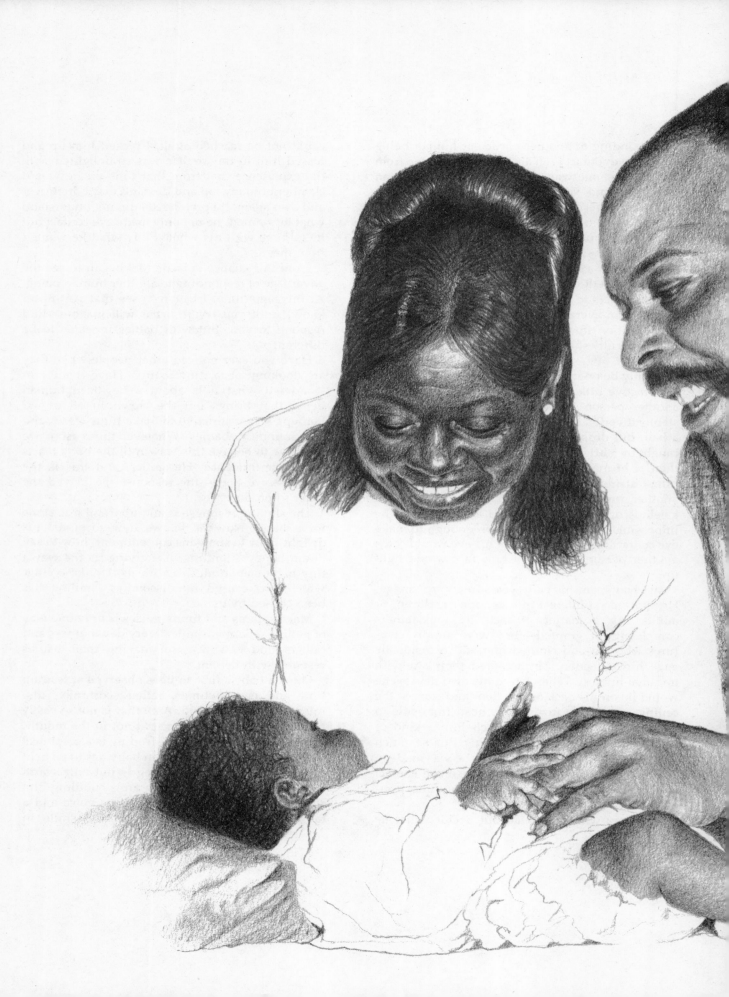

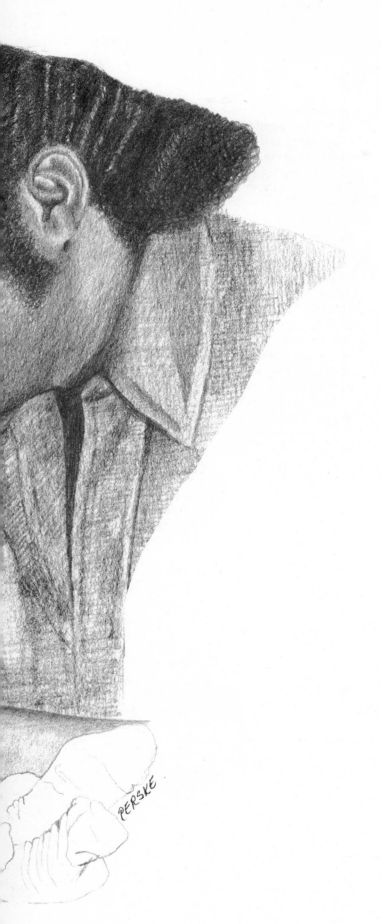

response. As Martin Grotjahn put it in his book *Beyond Laughter* (New York: McGraw-Hill, 1957):

> Only the human mother can look down on her suckling baby and smile at him in love. And only the human baby can have his mother in his mouth and look up and find her with his eyes. . . . This intimacy is typically and uniquely human.

This is the time of life when a baby's inborn sense of humor can be strengthened. Like smiling, it grows out of his awareness of the love that surrounds him. From this atmosphere comes a curious behavior, well-known to mothers throughout the ages, something called "breast-play."

It probably happens for the first time by accident. The hungry baby gropes around. With his mother's help he finds the nipple and sucks lustily. Then, for some reason or another, the nipple pops out of his mouth. For a moment the baby is merely bewildered. Then, as it begins to dawn on him that he has lost his life-giving nourishment, he begins to respond with anger and fear. But before he starts to cry, his mother puts the nipple in his mouth again. His relief is instantaneous. He suckles harder than ever before, and, as his eyes meet his mother's, they both laugh together. After this, the mother repeats the performance occasionally, pulling the nipple away and making him follow after it in a kind of loving tease so as to make him laugh with her again.

This kind of laughter—the laughing at fear—is the basis of humor and should be encouraged throughout the years. A sense of humor grows out of love and trust. It can be stifled very early in life by cold indifference. It can also be smothered by overprotection, which prevents the child from experiencing pain, fear, discomfort, and loss even in very small doses.

In the beginning of life, both laughter and tears have a place and a purpose.

One of the interesting things about the beginning of life is that it does not take place in a vacuum. All human babies, one way or another, have somebody to take care of them. This *somebody* is usually the mother, but it could be equally well a father, grandmother, sister, aunt, foster-mother, nurse, or whatever. Without this somebody the newborn human being would simply fade away and die. Babies cannot be thought of, or talked or written about without consideration of this other person. (In these pages this person, for the sake of brevity, is called the mother. For the same reason, all babies are referred to here as boys, "he" being used to mean both "he and she.")

Mothers sometimes feel very unprepared for motherhood, but the fact of the matter is that no mother can ever be totally prepared for her baby—no matter how many books she has read, or how many children she has had. This is because babies are individuals. Though they appear to act very much the same, actually they all respond slightly differently from one another. Every baby has individual needs that are peculiar to him. This applies equally to the slower-than-average as well as to the so-called average child.

It is very difficult for a mother to know whether she is helping her child develop or not, whether she is helping or hindering his progress, giving him too much or too little attention (like houseplants that wilt when they have too little water and also when they have too much). Can she tell how much is enough?

Unlike houseplants, babies are able to communicate with us. A mother's job is to find out what her baby is trying to tell her, so that she will know how much is enough. She does this by listening, watching, and observing his responses and reactions; by getting herself onto the same wavelength as her baby and tuning in to his world; by looking at it through his eyes, listening to it with his ears, touching it with his hands, and seeing it from his point of view.

This is the way that Billy and Jeff and Doug taught me to be a teacher. This is the way your baby teaches *you* to be a mother.

3. feeding is far more than food

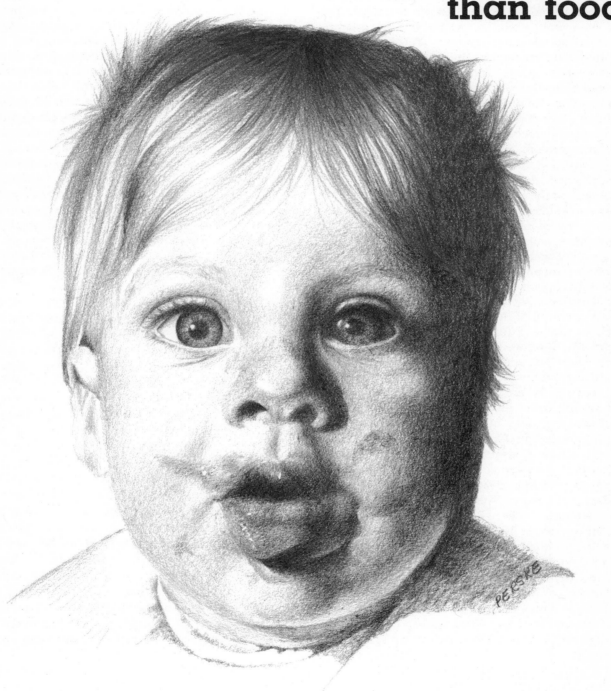

It has always seemed rather strange that the delight and pleasure of infant feeding, which was described in the last chapter, have produced so few psychological studies. In its intimacy, the involvement of a mother and her suckling baby is matched only by that of lovers. Yet *this* intimate relationship has almost been drowned in the oceans of research and study. However, the mother-child theme *has* provided inspiration for some of the world's most creative artists.

At any rate, the giving and taking of nourishment is only part of the mother-child relationship. As time goes on, and a mother tries to wean her baby and take him off the bottle or breast, she should try to retain as much as she can of the closeness of the involvement.

The way to do this is to make changes in the feeding procedure gradually, a small step at a time. Also, make only *one* change at a time. For instance, if your baby is used to being breast or bottle fed, do not expect him to be able to manage cereal in a spoon right away, both the spoon and the cereal being new things for him. Instead, give him a spoonful of liquid he is familiar with, and when he is able to deal with the spoon in this way, gradually introduce the cereal.

The same procedure applies when you feel he is ready to graduate from your lap to a high chair for his feeding. When you make this transition, do not introduce new foods or new utensils until he is quite used to and quite happy about his new seating procedure. Give him just *one* new experience at a time to deal with; he will find it much easier that way, and so will you. Also, when you begin to feed him away from you, remember to replace your close physical presence with your close attention so he will not feel that he is being cut off or rejected by you.

As he gradually learns to feed himself, he will become so absorbed in that process that he will not feel dependent on your attention. Then you can move away completely and let him manage alone. It will be a very messy affair at first and can best be dealt with by setting aside a corner of the kitchen where you can easily clean up spills.

At this stage of the game it is best not to interfere too much. Let him make his own mistakes, because he will learn from them. Avoid scolding over spills and messes. Wipe them up without comment. In the first place, they are bound to happen while he is learning, and in the second, you do not want him to feel he can attract your attention by doing something undesirable.

A word to the wise: Be careful when you scold your child. You may find he would rather be scolded than ignored. By scolding him, you may be encouraging him to repeat the action you were scolding him about in the first place.

For a child, then, eating and learning to feed himself can be accomplished best in a gradual way taking only one step at a time. Sometimes the procedure goes well, and he is happily accepted into the family mealtime circle. At other times problems crop up which can turn meals into battles, and parents discover how stubborn and difficult an otherwise cooperative child can become.

Man does not live by bread alone, but we all know that bread is the staff of life and that without food we starve. So there is understandable concern when a child refuses to eat. This is particularly true in the case of the child who happens to be developing slowly, because very often such a child is small for his age. Naturally there is anxiety when a smaller-than-average child balks at his food—for how else, the mother reasons, is he going to grow? Under these circumstances, is it better for her to force him to eat, or should she give in and allow him to go without his meal?

Perhaps the best way to answer that question is to go back to the beginning again—back to the baby who cries for attention, the baby who cries to tell his mother he is hungry. If, for the most part, he has been fed when he indicated he was hungry, it stands to reason his wishes should be respected when he points out that he is not. The best thing to do is simply put the food away and wait for the next meal. If he becomes hungry before the next meal, just give him a drink of water and nothing else. Most children can miss an occasional meal, and some can go without food for several days and come to no harm.

Some mothers find that they have a baby who is never really hungry. This happens often with retarded babies, and it does present an extremely difficult problem. When it is a question of the baby's losing weight or not being able to suckle properly, your physician should advise you what to do. If he should suggest force-feeding, here are a few hints which may prevent possible long-range problems.

First of all, make the whole affair as pleasant as possible. Try a little food often rather than a lot all at once. Keep *your* fears and frustrations in the background, remembering that babies have an uncanny way of knowing your feelings however well you hide them. Your goal is to make mealtimes enjoyable for both you and your baby.

If a child goes off his food all of a sudden, there is probably a good reason for it—perhaps a cold, a fever, teething problems. At these times children often prefer a soft or liquid diet, but this can lead to difficulties later on. Roddy had gone through an uncomfortable time when he was teething, refusing everything except liquids. By the time his teething problem had cleared up, he had got into the habit of eating only liquid foods and spitting out anything solid. He even got to the stage, a year or so later, where he would struggle to prevent his mother from putting a toothbrush into his mouth!

Debby's feeding problem began when she choked on a crumb. She also happened to have a minor heart condition. When I knew her she had a full set of beautiful white teeth, but she would only eat food that had been pulverized in a blender. Her mother told me that even a little string of celery would cause her to gag and choke. Knowing about her heart, her entire family was naturally upset. Under these circumstances, you can imagine my surprise when, at snack time, Debby snatched and ate with relish the cookie belonging to the child she was sitting next to!

How easy it is to underestimate the intelligence of those who are mentally retarded! Debby, who was the youngest in her family, was a child with Down's Syndrome. She had discovered the most effective way to become an instant celebrity in her family. When nobody was taking any notice of her at mealtimes, she would begin to gag and choke and immediately she would be the center of loving and concerned attention.

The need to attract attention is a strong motivating force in children. This means they will go to great lengths to create attention—just as Debby did. Here was a little girl—at the time of the stolen cookie she was only just beginning to walk—who had deliberately changed the normal pattern of eating in order to become the center of attention. She had not brought about this state of affairs entirely on her own, of course—she had been aided and abetted by her family. The first time she gagged and choked on a crumb of solid food they were afraid she might affect her heart and from then on they fed her only liquid food. They did not realize that coughing up or gagging is the natural way of dealing with food that has been swallowed before being properly chewed up. (As a matter of fact, according to Edmund S. Crelin, in the very young child, the opening at the back of the mouth is relatively larger than it is in an adult—so a baby is *less* likely than an adult to suffer disastrous consequences from choking.)

By the time a baby starts getting teeth, he is ready to be introduced to food that has to be chewed. In fact, one way to help the teething process is to hold a hard crust of stale bread in his mouth so he can help the tooth come through the gum by chewing down on the rusk. This eases the pain of the emerging tooth and at the same time encourages the proper chewing and grinding motion.

There is a very particular reason that children who have Down's Syndrome should learn how to chew. Often these children have rather protruding tongues. In order to chew, of course, they have to push them back into their mouths. Thus chewing helps the child control his tongue.

Learning to deal with different kinds of food can come about only if the child is given the experience of eating a variety of things. Taste is the main property associated with food, and commercial baby food and foods pulverized in a blender do give the child a variety of taste experiences. But there is a bland uniformity to the texture. To the developing child, texture is far more important than taste.

The only way a child can learn to deal with texture is by the actual experience of eating a variety of foods. The reason for this is that the child has to change these different textures into a consistency that he can swallow easily. He has to learn by experience that some foods have to be chewed for a long time before they can be swallowed (raw apples), whereas others, like toast or cookies, dissolve much more quickly in his mouth. Bread, potatoes, meat, cheese, bananas, and oranges all have different textures; and he has to learn how to chew them up so that he can swallow them. We cannot teach him how to do this, but we *can* give him different textures to experiment with.

Experimenting with texture is important because biting, chewing, and swallowing all involve the use and control of many parts of the mouth, throat, and nose. The lips, tongue, teeth, jaw, soft palate, and the breathing mechanism all have to work together; and this coordination can only come about through constant practice. (The breathing mechanism is involved since you cannot swallow and breathe at the same time.)

Besides introducing the child to the texture of different foods, there are other ways to help him develop control over the various eating and breathing mechanisms. These other ways involve the various methods of receiving food.

In the newborn baby, the method is sucking on a nipple and swallowing. Consider the number of different muscles a baby has to use in order to suckle and swallow. Fortunately most babies are able to do this right away. Are they born with this ability, or do they learn it very quickly? Surely the baby's ability to suckle has something to do with the immediate satisfaction of warm milk in his mouth.

Once the baby can suckle and swallow with ease, he can be given an occasional sip of liquid from a spoon—orange juice, perhaps. This is different and a little more difficult for him to manage than sucking on a nipple. After this he can learn to eat solids from a spoon.

While he is becoming used to eating from a spoon, there are many things that can be done to help his development. Instead of just automatically giving him a spoonful of food every time he opens his mouth, leave the spoon an inch or so away so he will have to reach out for it. Put the spoon slightly to the side of his mouth so that he has to turn toward it. Introduce him to an ice cream cone and coax him to lick it with his tongue.

What you are doing is encouraging him to participate actively in the feeding process. This is a preliminary step to his learning to feed himself.

A suckling baby is held in a lying position, but when he begins to eat solids from a spoon, he should be placed in more of a sitting position. If he is not yet sure of himself sitting up, a good way to spoon-feed him is to set him on your lap facing away from you, so his back is supported against your chest. In this position you can eventually help him feed himself by having him hold onto the spoon with you. The easiest way is actually to enclose his hand in yours on the spoon. In this way you can encourage him gradually to take more initiative, and you will be able to tell when he is ready to do more of the job on his own. Sometimes the hardest task seems to be getting the food out of the bowl and onto the spoon. You can give him a hand with this part of the operation, and then let him bring the spoon up to his mouth on his own.

The same thing applies when he is learning to use a fork and knife, though by this time he may be big enough to resent your trying to help him and prefer to struggle with it on his own. Do not discourage him with negative verbal instructions such as: "Not that way . . . hold it the other way." He will only become confused. Instead give him plenty of opportunity to watch while the rest of the family are eating. Show him rather than tell

him. He will find it much easier to do what you *do* than to do what you *say*.

Trying out new tastes and textures and using different utensils are all important experiences quite apart from providing nourishment for the child. The experience of licking may have longer-lasting significance than the food value of the ice cream. The ability to suck through a straw may have greater implications than the thirst-quenching quality of the soda pop. Discovering how to eat cherries and grapes and learning to spit out the pits; chewing gum and trying to remember not to swallow it; sucking hard candy; crunching up nuts—all these things are new and interesting for a child, quite apart from satisfying his appetite. Only through actually doing them will he learn *how* to do them.

Temperature is something else a child learns about through eating. By sampling hot and cold foods, he will learn to blow on hot soup to cool it and discover what happens to an ice cube when he plays with it.

Eating various kinds of foods; dealing with new tastes, textures, and temperatures; and using different implements are ways children learn control over their various eating and breathing mechanisms. The interesting thing to note is that these same mechanisms also happen to be part of the vocal system. Learning to control them by the daily practice of eating will help the child when he eventually begins to talk. So, curiously enough, the better a child is able to cope with food and eating, the better prepared he will be to deal with talking.

Life for the slower-than-average child is full of difficulties, and it is natural for the parent to try to remove these difficulties for him rather than to help him overcome them. Mashing up food for a slower-than-average child so he will not have to try to deal with solids, though understandable, prevents the child from having experiences which will help him later on. In this case, it deprives him of experiences which will prepare him for talking. It is a short-term policy which does more harm than good. Gradual or step-by-step introduction to new things and experiences is what the parents of the slower-than-average child should keep in mind.

It is the same in all areas of growing up. A child learns by overcoming the difficulties of life. We can help him overcome those difficulties by breaking them down into small steps which he then learns to climb one at a time. For the slower-than-average child, the goal is not to do things for him, or to take away experiences which he finds too difficult, but to help him gradually, step by step, to do things for himself.

4. speech is more than mere words

Human speech sets people apart from other living creatures. However, this ability is only one way of communicating with others. Gesture and intonation, body language, and sounds often speak louder and more clearly, especially to children. The tone of voice, the expression on a face, and the touch of another person's hand tell a small child more than can be conveyed in mere words. As a result, little children are likely to copy sounds and gestures early in their development.

This was brought home to me some years ago when I was singing a nursery rhyme—I believe it was "Jack and Jill"—with a group of preschool children. Dennis, who was nearly four years old, had never attempted to say one single word to my knowledge, and hardly ever made any sounds either, and I was beginning to despair of his ever being able to do so. Jeremy, who was sitting across from Dennis, knew the words of the song well; but he was bored and restless and, instead of joining in, he made a sound known as the Bronx cheer or raspberry! This sound was echoed without hesitation by my silent little friend Dennis. His enormous grin of delight at his achievement made me realize that noises like this are far more interesting to the child who has not yet learned to speak.

After all, the world is full of curious and wonderful sounds—footsteps, opening doors, telephones, wind, rattles, birdsong, breathing, garbage cans, cars, water running, food frying, people talking—they are all new and exciting to the child. He has not learned, as he will when he grows older, to block out many of the surrounding noises and concentrate on one sound, particularly the sound of the human voice.

Human speech, at this point in a child's life, is simply a series of sounds (happy sounds to make him smile, scolding sounds to make him cry) too complicated for him even to try to imitate. On the other hand, he can cough, laugh, sneeze, belch, cry, gurgle, and coo. He will enjoy copying these sounds when you make them—even Bronx cheers! It becomes a game he plays with you as he repeats them over and over again.

Listening to you is a good habit for him to get into, for you can gradually introduce new and more meaningful sounds for him to imitate— sounds that can be connected to objects (animal noises, the ticking of a watch or clock, the ringing of a telephone, and so forth).

Next, you can encourage him to use conversational sounds and sounds that accompany gestures. These are the kinds of noises that people use all the time without perhaps even realizing it. The "ouch!" when you hurt yourself, the "oops!" when you make a mistake, the "uh huh" of agreement (usually combined with a nodding head), the "tut tut" meaning "fancy that!" or "oh dear!" or "I can hardly believe what you are telling me," the "uh uh" and a wagging finger which means "no" or "stop," and of course the "mmm mmm" that keeps conversation going.

Various sounds and gestures are used in different cultures, but most of them are universally understood. Certainly children who do not talk yet find them more meaningful and easier to copy than words. By using sounds and appropriate gestures, they are able to carry on a conversation without actually talking. Because some children are able to speak only after many years, it should be remembered that the goal of speech is to make people able to communicate with one another. If your child is able to do this more easily with gestures and sounds, it is better to help him communicate more effectively this way. It is better to help him do what he *can* do more effectively than to set goals so high he cannot possibly reach them.

This is not to say that a child who seems to be unable to talk should only be taught to use sounds and gestures. At all times the words he is trying to say should be repeated by you as he indicates his needs. Carry on a conversation with him and, if anything, use more words yourself. Constantly be alert for what he is trying to convey and, in simple terms, put it into words for him.

This means getting down to his level and seeing the world through his eyes. It is not something you expect to have to do *all* the time, but try to spend some time each day conversing one way or another with your child. It is better to give him your full attention for small amounts of time than to *be* with him all the time and yet never really communicate with him.

Even though it is hard to realize, children who do not know words nevertheless understand a great deal of what *we* are saying. They are able to do so because they interpret our gestures, our body language, and the tone of our voice long before they understand the words that accompany them.

Timothy—only just beginning to walk—has a favorite song. It is "If You're Happy and You Know It, Clap Your Hands." He cannot say any words yet, but he laughs with the greatest glee when I come to the line "If you're mad and you know it, stamp your feet," and I put on my angriest face while I sing the words. It is the same angry face he sees when I am scolding him for pouring sand over another child's head in the sandbox. Yet he laughs at my make-believe anger, and he respects it when it is real. Even without understanding words, he is well aware of this subtle difference and shade of meaning.

For a child like Timothy, who cannot talk yet and may not be able to for some years to come, his problem is *not* in understanding the world around him—it is in having other people understand *him*. We are so used to the idea of human speech that many of us do not appreciate the intelligence of a child who cannot talk. Yet, as Timothy showed me, even without the use of words, he was capable of a high degree of understanding. How unfortunate it is that the capability of an individual is so often measured by his ability to use words.

If Timothy, as a toddler, can tell the difference between truth and make-believe, surely we should not worry about his inability to say words yet. Let us build on the abilities he already possesses. He can tell reality from pretense—can he see the difference between up and down, in and out, over and under, stop and go, "throw it on the floor" and "pick it up," "pull it out of the

closet" and "put it away," "pull your socks on" and "take your socks off"?

These are the ideas to use in daily contact with Timothy and children like him. Though we will be talking all the time, appropriate gestures should be added to point up what we are saying. In time, Timothy will copy our gestures and begin to associate them with our words. As he hears them repeated over and over he may, in time, attempt to say them himself.

As he begins to recognize the difference between things, he will start to notice similarities—not similarity of words; that comes much later in life—for example, the reflection of a familiar face in a mirror, the similarity between a picture and the object it represents.

Cindy stroked her hair and pointed to her feet when she was shown pictures of a brush and comb and a pair of red shoes. She could not say the words, but she certainly recognized the objects in the pictures.

At about the same time in her life Cindy began to show an interest in matching things—that her hands matched her doll's hands, that both she and her mother wore hats, that one red shoe matched her other red shoe, and so on.

If your child enjoys looking at pictures and matching things, encourage him to point with his finger. If there is more than one object on a page, or if there are two shoes in front of him, have him point to each one separately. This will teach him to appreciate the difference between one object and another, as well as the difference between *one* thing and a whole lot of things. This, of course, is a beginning step to counting and understanding numbers.

Pointing to different parts of her body as we named them was something else that Cindy loved to do. She was able to do this long before she made any attempt to say the words herself. Children like her will be intrigued by the fact that they have *two* feet, hands, and ears and yet only *one* mouth and nose. You can point out many things in everyday conversation that will help your child to understand the idea of number.

PERSKE

"Take *one* cookie," "here are two apples—you may have one," "give Daddy one cake," "show me your shoe—you have two shoes, one . . . two."

When your child copies a sound you have made (like Dennis and the Bronx cheer) you have another opportunity to introduce numbers. Suppose he imitates a cough, for instance. Cough again deliberately, and if he copies it again you have a game going together. See what he will do when you cough twice in succession. You can do the same thing knocking on a door; can he copy the number of times that you knock? Banging on a drum is great fun; see what happens when you bang the drum many times. What you are doing at this stage is pointing out the difference between one sound and two sounds, one thing and a number of things.

Singing is probably the way a little baby begins to *enjoy* words—listening to them as beautiful sounds. There is something soothing and yet stimulating in hearing songs repeated over and over. Many children find it easier to sing words than to say them. Others have a whole repertoire of songs before understanding any of the actual words. Many children who do not or cannot sing love to join in with actions such as hiding their hands behind them and pointing one at a time for "Where Is Thumbkin?" or pretending to wash their faces and brush their teeth for "This Is the Way We Wash our Face."

Songs—and the best are the old ones familiar to everyone—are the way a child is introduced to his literary heritage. Nursery rhymes, folk songs, and familiar hymns need to be woven into the fabric of his being at an early age because this is one way of passing the cultural background from one generation to the next. Television, radio, and records can help here; but so often in these media the new and innovative is emphasized at the expense of the old and familiar. The result, for the slower-than-average child, is that instead of learning to join in with songs everyone knows, which would help him integrate more with society, he learns only the latest hit tunes, which, by the time he has learned them, will have become out-of-date and forgotten. Slower-than-average children take longer to learn songs. Because of this it is better to teach them the type of song that will be suitable for them later on, when they are grown up. This means including old favorites such as "I've Been Working on the Railroad" or "Row, Row, Row Your Boat" or "Daisy, Daisy" along with nursery rhymes.

Sometimes it is quite hard to remember all the old songs that you were brought up with. This is where grandmothers and grandfathers come into the picture, for they probably remember singing to you when you were a baby and can teach the same songs to their grandchildren.

While your child is listening to people singing and talking, he will discover one day that things and people have names. People to begin with—you to begin with. In nearly every language "ma-ma" is one of the first words a youngster says, and in nearly every language this word means mother. Perhaps this is because "mm-mm" is one of the first sounds of contentment a baby makes.

It is rather difficult for parents to accept the fact that, when their child begins to use words or sounds that represent words, he may not really understand what he is saying at all. Our son's first word was "car"—at least that is what I fondly imagined, and I even recorded the date in my baby book. Looking back, I realize he probably had no idea what he was saying on the first occasion. It simply happened that he made a "ca" sound while watching his father come up to the house in the car. We had waited so long for this first word! I grabbed him, hugged him, and raced out to tell my husband the good news. For the next few weeks, I remember, Alan called everything "car."

It is easy to confuse children this way. I should have kept my enthusiasm and pleasure to myself and encouraged him to play with his new sound, to make a game of it with me. Something like this:

Alan: ca ca
Me: ca ca
Alan: ca ca
Me: ca ca ca ca
Alan: ca ca ca
Me: car (going to the car and pointing to it)
Alan: car
Me: da da car
Alan: da da
Me: Daddy's car
And so on.

Being able to say something which somebody else understands is an exciting event for both the speaker and the listener, particularly if the speaker is doing it for the first time. The first time for Dennis happened one day when he began to do a peculiar little dance all by himself in the corner of the room. He kept repeating an unintelligible babble, and it was only when we saw he had put the candlestick on the floor that we recognized the tune as "Jack Be Nimble, Jack Be Quick." Then, as we watched him, he jumped right over the candlestick, leaving no doubt in our minds he knew exactly what he was saying.

Meanings and words do not always fit together quite so well. Whenever Roddy washes his hands he says, "Hot, cold, hot, cold, hot, cold"!

Conversations with children like Alan, Dennis, and Roddy are on two levels. Because they are beginning to experiment with consonant sounds and words, we must encourage them to try more of these sounds. But, at the same time, we must continue to stimulate them with the ideas, concepts, and discriminations which were discussed earlier in the chapter. What has to be remembered with slower-than-average children is that understanding is a separate skill which has little to do with the formation of recognizable words.

The ability to produce words depends on the operation of the many different parts of the mouth, throat, tongue, lips, lungs, etc. that make up the vocal mechanism. Learning to use the vocal mechanism is a long and complicated process. It takes a great deal of practice. The average baby spends an enormous amount of time vocalizing in the form of cooing, shrieking, crying, screaming, gurgling, chuckling, etc.

As a newborn baby, he uses these sounds to communicate his moods and feelings—crying because he needs something, laughing with joy and delight. But there comes a stage later on when he makes sounds and noises for the pure pleasure of hearing his own voice. This stage also comes to the slower-than-average child, but it comes later in life, when the child is no longer a baby, and it lasts for a much longer time.

It can be a very irritating time for parents who misinterpret these vocalizations and do not understand the child's need to try out the sounds he can make. Liza discovered one day how to shriek. To her it was a wonderful sound, and it had a magnificent effect on all those around her. Everyone stopped what he was doing to look at her, and that made her do it more than ever.

It was only natural that Liza's family would assume that she "only does it to annoy, because she knows it teases," to paraphrase the Duchess in Alice's Adventures in Wonderland. They tried scolding her, but this did not stop her—and anyway they did not want to discourage her from making sounds. So they decided to pretend they did not hear her shrieks, and instead they began to make other sounds and noises such as barking and mooing to play along with her. In time, she began to enjoy copying these new sounds.

With the slower-than-average child the important thing is to encourage vocalization. This gives him the practice he needs in order eventually to begin to use words. The way you can do this depends on your imagination, but whenever you are alone with him, sing or make noises or play with sounds together. Make it an enjoyable and amusing experience for both of you.

Unfortunately, slower-than-average children can be put off when too much is demanded from them. Amy, at four years of age, was just beginning to use a few words, and her father and mother were delighted. Her grandmother was a teacher of the old school, who believed she could help Amy by sitting down and working intensively with her. This she did on several occasions. Shortly after this Amy's mother noticed that she was beginning to stutter mildly—and the stutter only happened to Amy when she was taken to visit her grandmother!

Therese was a plump little girl who really enjoyed food. She was in the habit, at mealtimes, of pointing to whatever she wanted because she could not talk. Eventually she began to say a few words. Her parents decided to try to speed up her talking. When she pointed to something she wanted at the dinner table, they insisted she make an attempt to say the word before they passed the food to her. For a few days all seemed to be going well, and Therese began to repeat one or two words. But then she did something that she had not done for several past months. She began to wet herself. Her mother could not understand it, but her father wondered whether they were putting too much pressure on her to talk. They decided not to be quite so insistent with her, and sure enough, in a few days, she was as well toilet-trained as she had been before.

There is a very thin line between having a child do as well as he possibly can and pushing him beyond his capacity. One of the best ways to be sure that you are not putting too much pressure on your child is to be on the watch for signs such as Amy's stutter or Therese's wetting. These signs may be outward indications of inward frustration.

Once children begin saying words, the important thing to do is to talk to them. Conversation is the way children learn how to use words. It is one thing to learn the names of people, objects, numbers, colors, sizes, and actions; but only in conversation do these words begin to have real meaning.

When you carry on a conversation with a child you should try to give him opportunities to use those words he knows best. Do not be discouraged if your child keeps saying the same word again and again. Eloise had a favorite word—kittycat—and every day she found all kinds of reasons for saying the word over and over until her family complained that she never said anything else. Favorite words can be used by adults to enlarge a child's vocabulary.

Eloise's love of cats can be used to teach her how to use more words. The way to do this is to build up conversations around her particular interest. When Eloise begins looking for her cat, her parents should say such things as "Where do you suppose Kitty is?" "Is he behind the sofa?" "Who is that under the bed?" "What is Kitty doing?" "Isn't he soft and cuddly?" and so on. Out of these kinds of (rather one-sided) conversational questions Eloise may begin to put *kitty* together with another word such as "kitty bed" or "kitty soft" or "kitty where?" and thus begin to converse. The idea of "yes" and "no" can be introduced here: "Kitty on the bed?" "No, Kitty's not on the bed." "Yes, Kitty is in the closet."

Conversations with beginning talkers consist mainly of questions which give the child a chance to use his favorite word as the answer. Adult: "What's under the bed?" Eloise (triumphantly): "Kittycat!"

At this stage correct pronunciation is less important than the attempt to say words. Children can be put off if their efforts are misunderstood or ridiculed. Whenever possible simply accept what the child says, and, if you can, correct it by repeating the word properly.

Billy, for some reason or another, used a *Y* sound at the beginning of his words—"yookies and yuice" for "cookies and juice." Obviously he was able to make the *c* sound, but "yookies" seemed to come more easily to him. We tried to correct the habit by pointing out things beginning with the *c* sound such as cat, camel, kangaroo, catch, car, kick. I shall never forget his amazement and then his burst of delighted laughter when he came across an animal in an alphabet book called a yak.

Books make it possible to show the whole world to your child while he is sitting on your lap. Unlike television or everyday experience, books can be looked at over and over again whenever you feel like it. Every page in a book may be different, but it never changes from one day to the next. For a child, there is something very reassuring about the rediscovery of a familiar book,

something stimulating about anticipating the story, about revisiting a world that stays the same forever.

Books for little children should be chosen with care. Pictures should be clear and precise. The more realistic they are, the easier it is for a child to relate them to his everyday experience, even though he will be constantly coming across things that he has never actually seen in real life. Wild animals, farm animals, birds, and insects for city children; fire engines, smokestacks, and skyscrapers for country youngsters. All these strange and unfamiliar things become part of a child's life and experience through books.

The text of a book is as important as the pictures. Except for simple counting and alphabet books and books of pictures, choose books with texts that appeal to you. *You* are the one who has to do the actual reading, and it is your interest that will stimulate your child.

Try to find books with clear pictures, interesting texts, and not too many words on each page. Little children find it hard to sit still and listen for too long, and they usually enjoy the activity of turning the pages over one by one.

As you read the same book over and over again, your child will begin to memorize the simple text. Soon he will be able to say some of the words along with you, and eventually he will be able to look at the book all by himself and your words will echo in his mind as he does so.

While you are reading you can encourage him to talk by asking him questions about the pictures and having him point to things he knows. Discussions about the pictures can introduce counting, colors, sizes, and shapes. Conversation about the story—what is happening and what is going to happen—encourages the child to join in the reading experience. It is *not* reading, but it does set up good habits for reading later on (sitting still, concentrating on one page at a time, taking an interest in the unfolding story, listening to your voice, and learning to tell the difference between the printed word and the pictures).

It is hard for adults to realize that, just as a baby

becoming aware of human speech is unable in the early stages to understand the words being spoken, so an older child, seeing printed words in a book, may not know what they are. For him written words and letters are simply squiggles. It will be many, many years before he is able to distinguish and recognize words and begin to read them for himself.

Meantime the important thing for him to learn is that the written word is different from a picture (or even from an object), even though it stands for the same thing. The word *shoe* means the same thing as the shoe in the picture; the word *milk* tells what is contained inside the carton; *John* is his name; etc. This is not reading, but it is laying the groundwork for future reading by showing the child that our world is full of things which stand for something else.

The same idea, of course, applies to numbers: 1, 2, 3, 4, 5, etc. are symbols which stand for something else. It is less important for a child to recognize these symbols than to understand what they stand for. So a child beginning to use words can be taught to count how many blocks, how many fingers, how many shoes, how many people by the actual experience of pointing to a series of objects one by one, and saying "One, two, three . . ." along with you. Eventually he will recognize the symbols; but, like recognition of letters and words, this comes later on in his life.

The beginning talker learns words not by seeing them written down, as adults do, but by hearing them spoken. So writing words on bits of paper and sticking them on familiar objects does not help children talk. Children learn to say words only when they hear words spoken.

You may find that your child makes certain sounds much more than others. And he makes these same sounds more frequently than any others. This was the case with Catherine, who went through a stage of making a lot of guttural gu-gu sounds. Because she was slow at talking (she was six at the time) her mother decided to fit words into these gu-gu sounds that she seemed to find easy to make. "Good girl" was pretty close, so whenever Catherine did anything to merit it, her mother would say "Good girl," which of course Catherine promptly repeated. So if your child seems slow to talk, see if you can pick out the sounds he *can* make and build up words on these favorite sounds.

In all things it is much better to help your child improve what he is able to do than constantly try to get him to do something he cannot quite manage. By building on his abilities—expanding, enlarging and encouraging them, whether they consist of gestures, sounds, words, or phrases—you can show him how to reach the goal of speech, which is to make it easier for him to reach out and communicate with other people.

5. toilet
training

Like so many other things in life, toilet training is a skill that eventually becomes a habit. Different children acquire the skill at different times in their lives. Some learn it at a very early age with no difficulty at all, while others seem to take forever.

Curiously enough, different cultures expect their youngsters to be toilet trained at different ages. In northern European countries, children are expected to be trained much younger than in southern Europe; in the Far East at a much earlier age than in North America.

In all cultures, however, the slower-than-average child will take a longer time and find it more difficult than other children. Because of this, the earlier these children are started on a toilet-training program the better.

Like other areas, toilet training involves both the child and the mother (often the father too). Some people are quick to point out that when a child is being toilet trained early in life it is the mother who is being trained rather than the child. Of course, this is true—at least partly. In all areas of development mothers are being trained, or are learning, alongside their children, just as teachers are being trained by the students they teach. Just as I was trained by Jeff and Billy and Doug, so mothers are constantly learning together with their children.

It is very unlikely that any clues will be given by slower-than-average children indicating when they are ready to start toilet training. Usually they appear to have no interest in the procedure. For this reason most mothers make no attempt to train them until they are walking. As walking often comes later in life for these children, they may not be trained by the time they are old enough to attend school. This can be an embarrassment, since many teachers feel that toilet training is somewhat outside their sphere of responsibility.

Toilet training can be started when the child is able to sit up alone. He does not have to be able to walk. If he can sit comfortably on his own, he can be placed on one of those infant training seats that fit onto the regular toilet, or in a child's training chair.

A training chair is more practical because it can be put in a corner of the bathroom out of the way and the child can use it without holding up the rest of the family. Also it is safer because it usually has a tray which prevents him from falling out, and he can be left in it for short periods of time while his mother gets on with something else. It is a wise investment for the slower-than-average child because toilet training takes time, and he will be able to use the training chair until he grows out of it.

Before she plans to start the training program there are several things a mother can do to ensure its success.

First of all, she should make a note of the times during the day when she has to change the baby because he is wet or soiled. The way to do this is to check the diaper about every hour or so during the day, starting when your baby gets up in the morning and ending when you put him to bed at night. Make a chart something like the one below, either in a notebook or on a piece of paper you can fix on the bathroom wall.

Time	M	T	W	T	F	S	S
7:00 AM	W	W	W	W	W	bm	W
8:00	D	D	D	D	D	D	W
9:00	W	W	W	W	W	W	D
10:00	D	D	D	W	D	W	D
11:00	W			D	W	D	W	W
12:00	bm		W	bm	D	W	W
1:00 PM	D	D	D	D	W	D	D
2:00	W	W	bm	W	W	D	W
3:00	D	bm	D	D	D	W	D
4:00	D	D	W	W	W	W	bm
5:00	W	D	D	D	D	D	D
6:00	D	W	D	D	W	D	W
7:00	bm	D	W	W	D	bm	D

W = wet
D = dry
bm = bowel movement

Keep a chart like this for several weeks. It is for your information only, so do not worry about omissions. What you are trying to discover is when your child urinates during the day. And how often? Also, when during the day does he have a bowel movement?

After a few weeks, examine the charts and see if you can see any kind of pattern emerging. In the example above, for instance, the child was always wet first thing in the morning, but usually was dry an hour later and then usually wet by the following hour. Therefore, sometime between 8:00 and 9:00 he usually urinated. The next step is to get him onto the training chair just before he has to go. Check his diaper in the usual way at 8:00 and, if he is dry, set him in the training chair and keep your fingers crossed.

Success, of course, is when he actually performs in the chamber of the training chair. Show him that you are pleased, but do not expect him to realize what he has done. Do not scold him for mistakes, which, after all, are not really his fault, as he has to rely on you to anticipate his needs. There will be many times when you will not get him to the bathroom in time, and many times when he will not seem to want to go at all.

What you are trying to do, at this early stage, is to establish a routine in his life, to get him into the habit of going in the training chair at a regular time every day—and to get him into the habit of going in the training chair rather than his diaper. This he will not necessarily prefer, because he has become very used to wearing a damp diaper and he may even like it that way.

His reward for going in the training chair is your approval, so show him you are pleased each time. Also gradually try to get him to realize why you are pleased with him. At first he will not be aware of urinating or having a bowel movement. At this early stage children are not aware of their bodily functions. To them, these things just happen. It takes practice and time for them to learn that, to a certain extent, they can control these particular functions.

So praise him when he is successful, but do not overwhelm him with your enthusiasm—keep that for when he realizes what he has done. When he reaches *that* goal he can share your excitement and pleasure. From then on he will understand what you expect of him.

This goal may take years to reach. When it happened to Catherine she was a big girl—so big that she wore the largest disposable diapers on the market. If she was not trained soon, her mother was afraid that Catherine would grow out of them. She showed no interest in the training procedure, though she was big enough to sit on the regular-sized toilet seat. She had no interest at all until one day she became aware of the splashing sound as she wet in the toilet. As it dawned on her that she was making the sound herself, and as she caught her mother's eye and realized that she had heard it too, an enormous grin came over her face. From that time on, all her mother had to do was to say, "I'm listening, Catherine," and Catherine would make a great effort to do it over again.

It is a great help for slower-than-average children to be rewarded for a task well done. Parental approval and praise or even a small candy are helpful at first, but as the child grows in competence, these rewards should be gradually withdrawn so the child has a chance to learn the satisfaction of completing the task itself, just as Catherine did.

When your child is in the habit of performing in the training chair early in the morning or after breakfast or whenever it is, you will find it helpful to continue keeping the chart. Now it will read something like the one on page 41.

It can be seen from this chart that the child is beginning to get into the habit of going in his training chair each day after 8:00, after breakfast actually. He then stays dry until sometime between 10:00 and 11:00. So the next step is to place him in his training chair sometime after 10:00 each morning. Also it is beginning to look as if he generally has bowel movements in the morning. In the afternoon he is still always wet when he gets up from his afternoon nap at about 3:00, but he then seems to stay dry until sometime after 5:00;

so it might be a good idea to put him in his training chair before he has his supper at 5:30. Last, it will be seen from the chart below that the child either urinates or has a bowel movement approximately six or seven times each day. Therefore it is unnecessary to continue checking his diaper every hour or so, and from now on checks can be made every hour and a half, eventually every two hours.

Gradually you are getting the child into a routine of going on his training chair at regular intervals during the day. These intervals will depend more on your own daily schedule of events, meals, and responsibilities than on the clock.

Time	M	T	W	T	F	S	S
7:00 AM	bm	W	W	W	W	W	bm
8:00	D√	bm	D√	D√	D√	bm	D√
9:00	D	D	D	D	bm	D√	D
10:00	D	D	D√	bm	D	D	W
11:00	W	W	bm	D	W	W	D
12:00	D	D	W	W	D	D	D√
1:00 PM	W	W	D√	D√	W	W	W
2:00	D	D	D	D	D	D	D
3:00	W	W	W	W	W	W	W
4:00	D	D	W	D	D	D√	W
5:00	D√	D√	D	D	D√	D	D√
6:00	W	D	D	W	W	W	D
7:00	bm	W	W	D	D	D	W

W = wet
D = dry
bm = bowel movement
√ = performed in training chair

As he becomes more capable, you will find that you are saving quite a bit of time and money on washing and buying diapers. As he will be using the same diaper for a longer length of time, the cloth ones will be more practical because they can simply be unpinned and pinned on again. However, disposable diapers can be used if great care is taken to remove them, or if a roll of cloth tape is kept handy for when the diaper tapes lose their stickiness.

As he gets into the habit of performing in his training chair, your child will begin to take an interest in what is happening and gradually recognize that he does have a certain amount of control over these functions. During this time your attitude toward his successes and his mistakes should also gradually change. In the past, when he was wet or soiled, it was mainly because you had not put him on the training chair in time. But once he is in the habit of going to the bathroom at fairly regular intervals during the day, the responsibility for waiting for these intervals rests on his shoulders. You can feel quite justified in being annoyed with him for not waiting, though obviously you have to take into account such things as upset stomachs, diarrhea, or excessive liquid intake.

The question is how to present your righteous annoyance to your child in such a way that he will learn from it. Scolding is seldom effective because most children rather enjoy the attention of it. Spanking is not much use because most mothers hate to hurt their children, and if it does not hurt, the child obviously will not think of it as a punishment. The best way to punish a child is to ignore him!

The way to ignore a child who has a wet or soiled diaper is to change him without saying one single word to him and without once looking him in the eye. Most children *hate* this kind of treatment and will go to great lengths to prevent its happening again. After an accident, when he again goes properly in his training chair, remember to be ready with your praise and approval.

You may still find it helpful to continue keeping your charts, which will now look something like this:

Time	M	T	W	T	F	S	S
First thing when he gets up	W	W	W	bm	D	W	W
After breakfast	bm	√	√	√	W	W	√
Before lunch	D	bm	√	D	D	D	bm
Before nap	√	√	W	√	√	√	√
After nap	W	W	BM	W	BM	W	W
Before supper	D	D	W	√	W	√	√
After supper	√	W	√	D	√	D	W

W = wet
D = dry; put on training chair but doesn't go
√ = urinated
bm = bowel movement
BM = bm in training chair

On the chart you will see that though the child is still wet first thing in the morning and also after his afternoon nap, he is frequently dry just before lunch, indicating that he is nearly ready to cut out that session.

By the time your child has a chart that is similar to the one above, he will probably be walking. Instead of taking him to the bathroom automatically, what you can begin to do is to ask whether he wants to go or not. Use words that come naturally and easily to your family, but use phrases that are universally understood rather than baby words or pet names. Say, "Do you want to go to the bathroom?" or "Do you have to pee?" or whatever.

Eventually the great day comes when you find that the child no longer has any wet diapers during the day. Then your child can go with you to the store to buy his very own training pants. Do not worry if he still has to wear diapers at night or when he sleeps during the day, because control during sleep often takes a bit longer.

Now that he is wearing training pants he can begin to learn to take them down at the appropriate time and pull them up again. He can get into the habit of washing and drying his hands. He can begin to flush the toilet himself. If your child is a little boy, he can watch his father or his older brother and begin to stand up to urinate. Eventually, of course, you want him to be able to tell you when he has to go to the bathroom and after that to be able to go entirely on his own.

This all takes time and can be accomplished best only in a very gradual, step-by-step way. But every step the child takes gives him more independence and a satisfying feeling of accomplishment.

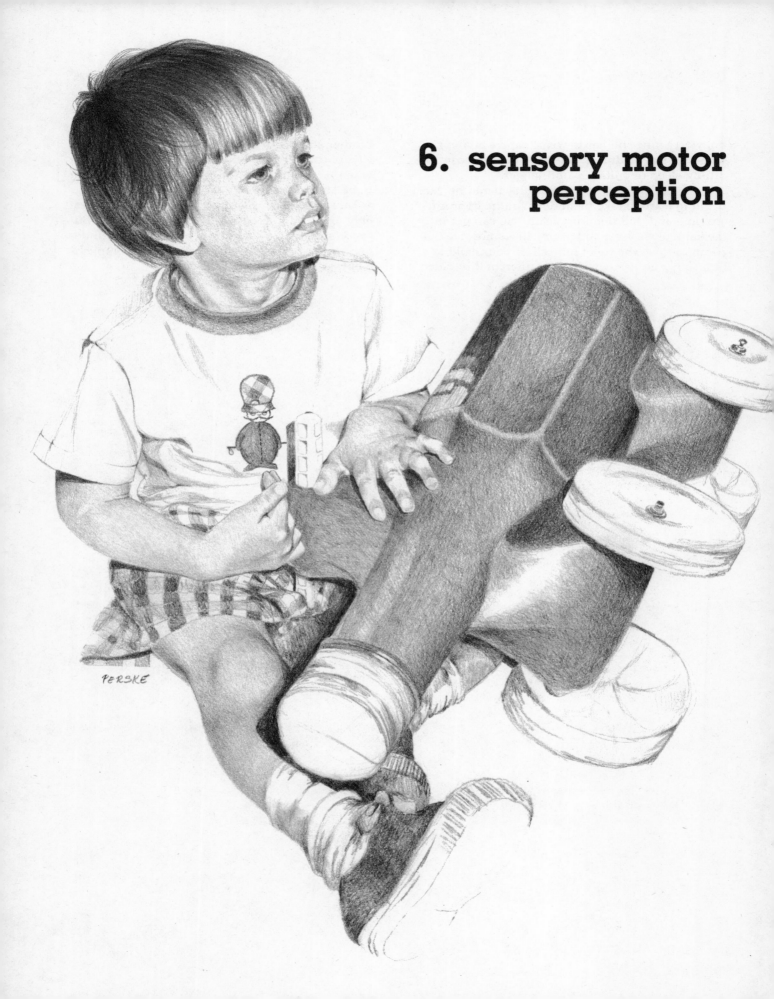

6. sensory motor perception

The title of this chapter is far less complicated than it sounds. *Sensory* refers to the five senses of touch, taste, smell, sound, and sight. *Motor* indicates movement. *Perception* is the ability to translate into knowledge information received by the senses.

Children from the moment they are born begin to perceive the world around them. During his waking hours, the young child uses his five senses to bring him information about his little world. At first his world consists mainly of himself and his mother. One of the first important tasks of his life is to find out about himself—his own body, what it is, what it can do, and how he can control it.

He does not know that it is his own voice he hears when he cries. He does not know that the hand he sees before his face belongs to him. He does not even realize, when a clear view suddenly appears in front of him, that it is because both his eyes have focused together at the same time.

Bringing the world into focus is probably achieved by a baby for the first time quite by accident. But once he has had that first clear glimpse of the world, he will want to make it happen over again. When we see a baby gazing apparently aimlessly into space, he is very likely trying to get his eyes to work together and bring him that clear picture one more time.

As young babies begin to see and to use their other senses to give them information, they begin to learn something of the nature of their world—how it looks, how it feels, how it tastes, how it smells, and how it sounds. As this is the way they learn, it is necessary to make sure that their senses are stimulated or kept active. Babies who are left alone in clean, white cribs in quiet, empty rooms have very little to tease or kindle their senses into response.

This does not mean that you have to be with your baby all the time (and of course, the clean, white crib in a quiet, empty room is the best place of all when the baby is asleep). But when the baby is awake, you should arrange his surroundings so that he has something to look at—a toy hung on the side of his crib or a mobile blowing in the breeze—and sounds to listen to, even if they are just the everyday household noises. As he learns to focus his attention on objects around him, he will be strengthening and learning how to use the tiny muscles that control his eyes.

Soon he will reach out with his hands to try to bring these objects close to him. This is not so much to see them better as to add to his store of knowledge by holding, touching, smelling, and tasting them. The way a young child does this is by putting things in his mouth.

The mouth, tongue, and lips are used by a child at this stage of life to tell him things that, as adults, we learn from our hands and other senses. In other words, the reason everything goes in his mouth is that this is how a young child learns about size, shape, texture, and taste. It is a completely natural and proper procedure—in time he will learn to use his hands to give him most of the same information, just as we do as adults.

Parents are sometimes embarrassed when their slower-than-average child who is no longer a baby still puts things in his mouth. They should try not to be angry with him, remembering that this is his way of learning. Instead they should teach him to feel with his hands, to smell with his nose, and to listen with his ears—in other words, to develop his other senses.

The way to do this is actually to guide the child's hand to stroke the cat's fur, feel the rough stubble on his father's face, touch the warm radiator, hold a hard pebble, clutch a wet sponge, and pop a soap bubble. And for listening, there are bells to ring, rattles to shake, mallets to pound, paper to tear, doors to slam, and kisses to blow. And as for smelling—well there are flowers and perfume, dinner cooking and coffee brewing, oranges and lemons.

As the child begins to see the objects around him more clearly, as he learns their properties through his mouth, his hands, his nose, and his ears, he is gradually building up a store of information about himself, about his surroundings, and about the people around him.

As he watches these people, he will want to

copy them; he will try to do what they do. His goal will be to stand up and walk like them.

This goal may appear to be easy to reach, simply because most children, in due course, do walk. But it is, in fact, a very complicated affair. To discover how complicated it is, just try to explain *in words* exactly how you get up out of bed in the morning. What is the very first movement that you make? What part of the body do you use? Which sets of muscles are brought into play? (As you think about your own body in this way, you become aware of the importance of knowing what each and every part of your body is capable of doing.)

If you had to make a mental list, in the correct order, of all the things you have to do in order to get out of bed before you actually got up in the morning, it might take you until lunchtime. So imagine how complicated it is for a child who does not even have the benefit of past experience to

draw upon. He has no way of knowing what each part of his body is capable of doing. He may not even be aware that his body belongs to him and that he can make it do what he wants.

At first, because newborn babies are so very dependent, they probably see themselves as mere extensions of their mothers. Therefore one of the first things a mother has to teach her baby is that he is, in fact, a separate and individual human being. In the beginning she can introduce him to his own body. She does this by playing little games with him—doing all the enjoyable things mothers have been doing throughout the ages with their babies. She tickles his tummy, she strokes his back, she plays "This Little Piggy"

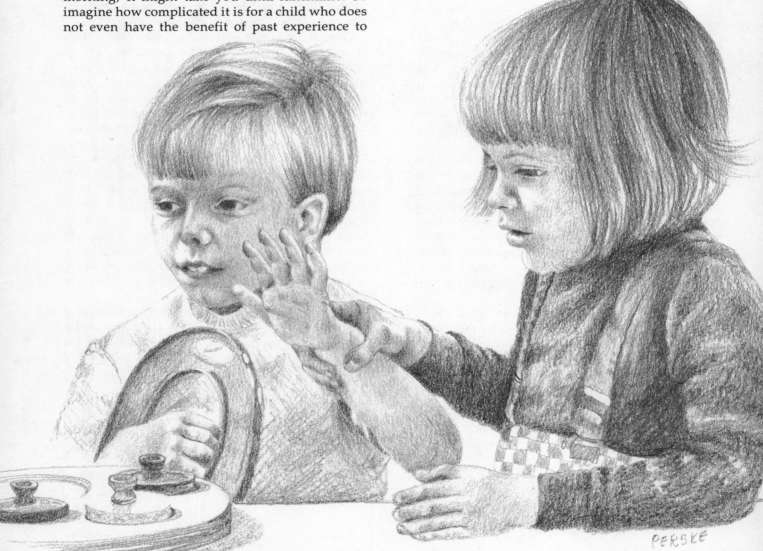

with his fingers and toes, she holds his tiny hands and pulls his arms gently to see how strong he is. She does all these things "for fun," but through this fun she teaches her baby about his own body.

To her surprise, a mother often discovers at this time that babies are not nearly so fragile as they look, even though they *are* extremely helpless. Obviously a baby can be hurt through carelessness, but he can take—and enjoy—quite a bit of rough-and-tumble treatment. This is where the father comes into the picture, because he can teach his child so many things from rough-and-tumble play. He can toss him up in the air, he can jog him around the room on his shoulders, he can roll him on the floor and generally play rough with him.

This kind of play activity is something all children need and love, and at the same time it teaches them so many new things. They learn about height and depth, about speed, about control and balance—all things they need to know in order to develop and progress.

There is only one thing to watch out for: be sure that your child is, in fact, enjoying the experience. If he is frightened, you must reassure him. If he does not like your roughness, go easy; try an activity that is a bit gentler. To have fun together, take your cue from the child—do not get him overexcited; do not play with him if he is overtired, or if it is just before bedtime when he needs to be calmed down and relaxed.

As time goes on and your child begins to crawl on his stomach and after that to creep on all fours, he will want to explore. Inevitably he will get into difficult situations. You will look around and find him teetering on the edge of the sofa, or stranded halfway up the stairs. Because it is possible he *could* fall off the sofa, and he *might* tumble down the stairs, one's natural inclination is to snatch him away from these dangers. But it is far better to hide your concern and go and stand quite calmly nearby, close enough to catch him if necessary. Then wait and see how he will extricate himself. You may be surprised to see how cleverly he manages to clamber back to safety on the floor. On the other hand, he may see you and put his arms

out to indicate he wants to be picked up. Try to resist doing this and instead show him, by actually putting his arms and legs in the right places, how to get down. This way you will be teaching him how to solve a difficult problem and also how to use his own body.

It is very tempting, when children get to this exploring stage, to prevent them from "getting into things" by putting them into playpens and baby-walkers. There is nothing wrong with either of these pieces of equipment. It does not do a child any harm to spend some time in them each day. But do not let your child stay in a playpen or a walker for too long. It is acceptable to confine him when you are preparing a meal or doing something that needs your complete attention, and for short lengths of time it will not hurt him; but used too much, both of these devices discourage the child from learning.

A young mother I once knew had her child use a baby-walker. Her little girl loved it. She thoroughly enjoyed walking around the house secure in the walker, which not only made it possible for her to sit down when she became tired, but also prevented her from bumping into things and from falling down. Because she liked to be in the walker, and because her mother saw no harm in it, she spent most of her waking hours in it. Finally her parents decided to see if she could walk on her own. They found that she was perfectly capable of walking alone, but they were dismayed to discover that she hurt herself by walking into the furniture and bumping into doorways. The reason for this was that she had never learned by experience how to avoid bumping into things. The walker had always absorbed the bumps before and prevented her from being hurt.

Perhaps it sounds rather cruel, but a few bumps and bruises are a small price to pay for a learning experience. Falling down and getting bumped are part of life for the toddler—he will take them all in his stride unless he is taught to make a great fuss over them.

Timothy—the little boy who thought it was so

funny when I pretended to be angry—was clambering up some steps in the nursery when he lost his balance and fell—plonk!—down on the floor beside me. He began to cry, so I picked him up to comfort him. This did not help matters at all because now he cried more than ever. In fact, after a while he became almost hysterical, and finally I had to tell him very firmly, "Stop it at once!" And he did. I put him down on the floor, and two minutes later he was back climbing up the steps again. Sure enough, he did the same thing as before—he lost his balance and fell down. His face crumpled up, but before he started to cry he looked around to see if I was watching. I pretended not to see him. Out of the corner of my eye I saw him choke back his tears, pick himself up and—you guessed it!—clamber right back up those steps again. When I told his mother she said: "Oh I always pretend not to notice when he falls and bumps himself. If he knows that I've seen him, he makes the most terrible fuss."

In learning to walk there is a fairly consistent sequence of events. The tiny baby begins by learning to control his neck and shoulder muscles so that he can hold his head up. Then he has to be able to operate his back muscles so that he can sit up properly. After that his legs and arms come into play so he can crawl on his stomach. He then begins to support his weight on his knees and wrists and creeps on all fours. He finds the way to pull himself up to a standing position. Next he learns to shove his weight back onto his legs and thighs so as to stand up on his own. Finally comes the first tentative step forward, and at last he walks alone.

Each of these stages or steps prepares the child for the one that comes next. The better the child is at any one stage, the easier it will be for him to manage the one that follows.

This means that if your child is slow to begin walking, the best way to help him is to make sure that he is as good as he possibly can be at all the previous tasks of sitting, creeping, crawling, pulling himself up, and standing on his own. It will not hurt a bit to have him practice doing these things over again. The more graceful and rhythmic he is about crawling and creeping, the more likely he is to be graceful and rhythmic about walking.

Paula and Micky were both unsteady on their feet and therefore their walking was very awkward. They both tended to fall over if they received the slightest shove, or bumped into the smallest obstacle. And they both fell heavily and awkwardly and hurt themselves. While I was trying to get them to practice some of the earlier stages, I discovered that Paula was not able to creep on all fours and Micky could not stand up without pulling himself up by holding onto a piece of furniture or somebody's hands.

Perhaps Paula's unsteadiness was caused by her not having developed enough strength in her knees and wrists. This kind of strength builds up automatically through creeping on all fours. Perhaps she was unsteady standing up because of the weakness in her knees, and she was fearful of falling (which made her more unsteady) because her wrists were not strong enough to break her fall. Micky's unsteadiness may have been the result of weak thighs and leg muscles, which would naturally gain strength the more he practiced standing up on his own.

It was easy enough to find a game to play which would encourage Paula to exercise on all fours; she thoroughly enjoyed pretending to be a horse racing around the room. But making it fun for Micky to stand up on his own was more difficult. In fact, there did not seem to be a way to make it enjoyable for him. The only way to help him seemed to be to put him on all fours in the middle of the room, away from the furniture, and then to stand behind him and pull his hips back and up so that he had to stand up. Eventually, after he was given a great deal of encouragement and praise, Micky learned to do it entirely on his own.

Catherine ("I'm listening, Catherine") was a very careless walker. She would trip over other children or toys on the floor, apparently not even noticing they were there. But despite this carelessness, she never once lost her balance. The other children might get hurt, the toys might get broken, but she never fell over. She also liked to clamber all over the jungle gym, but she was equally careless about that and had to be closely watched so she would not fall and hurt herself. In an effort to teach her to take care, I placed her on her stomach on top of an overhead horizontal ladder. In order to get down to the floor from this position she really had to think about what she was going to do. It was the same kind of situation as that of an adult thinking about every step of getting out of bed. What arm or leg was she going to move first, and where would she put it? At first she had to be helped. She had to be shown exactly where to place her arms and legs. But after she had done it a few times it became a challenge to her to see if she could do it on her own. She no longer had to be watched closely, because she had learned to be careful. In much the same way she learned how to walk along a balance beam without falling. Soon she began to enjoy the challenge of avoiding the other children and the toys on the floor. At this stage she was beginning to discover the secret of *graceful* movement.

Graceful, easy movement with an economy of effort is the goal to set for all children, whether they are crawling, creeping, walking, climbing, or running. Years ago, I remember a professor telling a group of physical education teachers: "You don't need to know his I.Q. to tell a child is slow. You can tell by the way he walks." Unfortunately this is often the case. Slower-than-average children often do not walk with the same ease, do not move with the same speed and grace as other children. The reason for this may be that parents and teachers are so concerned about the intellectual ability of the slow child that they fail to recognize the importance of the whole area of physical development.

In the young child, physical development and mental or intellectual growth go hand in hand. In the young child, learning—which is the acquisition of knowledge—can come about only through physical activity. The young child has five ways of receiving information—sight, sound, touch, taste,

and smell. In order to see properly he has to control his eye muscles. In order to hear he has to know how to turn his head in the right direction. He has to reach out with his hands in order to touch things, to bring them to his mouth in order to taste them; and he has to breathe in so that he can smell them. All these are physical activities.

By the time we become adults, we do not think about the physical aspect of using our five senses, because by that time they are so well attuned to the rest of our body that we use them without even thinking about them. However, when I became middle-aged I started to do something that made me think about one of my senses again—the sense of sight. I became a bird watcher. Bird watching made me realize that seeing can still be refined, even at a stage in life when one is beginning to need glasses. I began to observe birds, to distinguish one species from another. Later on I found I could even see them on the wing and I could identify them as they flew past. This ability—to recognize a bird as it flies—took years of practice. This practice involved my eyes and my ability to control them, to focus them on a moving object and keep that object in view long enough to be able to identify it. This ability to control the muscles of the eyes is exactly the same ability that young children have to learn. The world for young children is like the world of the non–bird watcher—full of birds they cannot see. If you never noticed a single bird in your entire life it probably would not matter much, but how are we going to find ways to show our children all the other wonderful things there are in this world?

A tiny baby banging the toy dangling on his crib, an infant feeding himself with a spoon, and a child pulling off his shoes and socks are all using perhaps the most important tools they have—their own hands and fingers. Learning to use hands and fingers constructively, carefully, and creatively takes years and years of practice. Many adults faced with a new project such as typing, sewing, carpentry, or playing the piano or a stringed instrument feel "all thumbs." If we think of children as also being all thumbs it will be easier for us to understand the problems they have when they are learning to perform even the very simplest tasks.

Slower-than-average children seem to have more difficulty than most with such things as taking their shoes and socks off (and even more with putting them back on again), getting their coats on and off, putting hats on (pulling them off seems to be much easier), getting in and out of their underclothes. It is much easier to show your child how to do these things if you have first discovered how you yourself would go about the task. Which hand goes where? Where do you put your fingers? Where does the thumb go? Only when you are sure of the way you do it can you set about showing your youngster how he can do the same thing.

Every day as you dress and undress your child, try to teach him to do more and more things for himself. Every time he goes to the bathroom he can be taught to pull his pants down and then pull them up again. When he lies down for his nap he can learn to take his shoes and socks off, and when he gets up he can "help" you put them on him. Soon he will take pride in doing these things on his own.

Tasks which involve picking up or holding onto very small objects, such as the tab of a zipper, are not possible for a child to accomplish until he is able to grasp properly with his thumb and forefinger. Before he learns this pincer grip, as it is called, he picks up small objects by grasping them between the tips of his fingers and the heel or cushion of his thumb. Watch your child and see how he picks up a slice of banana, a candy, a small cracker. If he still uses all his fingers and the base of his thumb you can help him to develop the proper grasping motion. A good way to do this is to give him a handful of dried beans and a wine bottle. You may have to show him what you want him to do at first, but most children seem to enjoy dropping the beans into the bottle, if only because of the nice sound it makes. It is very good practice because he learns he has to pick up and drop only one bean at a time. Eventually he will find that the only effective way to do this is to use the proper forefinger-and-thumb pincer-grip.

Once he can grasp small objects properly this way, he is ready to learn more complicated skills. He is ready to zip up and zip down, to snap fasteners together, to thread shoelaces, to button and unbutton, to buckle a belt, and so on. These things require greater precision and the ability to see what has to be done. No longer can you teach your child by showing him how you do it. Now he has to see for himself what has to be done, and he has to make his fingers perform the task. In other words his eyes see the hole in the shoe and also the lace, but his hands have to do the threading. His eyes see the button and the buttonhole, but his fingers have to push the button through.

This coordinated effort takes a great deal of practice to perfect. Most of us forget the difficulties of coordinating the hands, fingers, and eyes because we have done these everyday things so many times before. Only when something new comes along are we reminded how complicated it can be. Remember the first time you threaded a needle? Knotted a bow tie? Used chopsticks?

Slower-than-average children will find it even harder than usual to get their hands to do what their eyes show them has to be done. There are many kinds of toys and games which will encourage them to practice eye-hand coordination: stringing beads, building towers with blocks, putting different shapes into matching holes, working on jigsaw puzzles, nesting hollow boxes, stacking different-sized rings in the correct sequence, and so on.

At first you will have to show your child how to do these puzzles and games—how to string the bead and where to place the block, which hole matches which shape, and so forth. However, the goal of all this activity is not the same for you as it is for your child.

The goal or point of these games for the child is to make a necklace, knock over a tower of blocks, put in the last piece of a jigsaw puzzle so the complete picture can be seen—in other words, finish the task.

The goal for parents is quite different. It is to have the child learn from his play how to use his hands and fingers together, how to perform the task that he sees has to be done, how to teach himself to be better coordinated.

The kind of playthings you give your child depends upon his ability (what he can do) and also upon his interests (what he *likes* to do). Add to these two criteria a further consideration: what *you* think he should be learning while he is playing. Start off with simple playthings, the kind which have a few, large, easily handled pieces. As he becomes more capable he will enjoy the challenge of the same kinds of games and puzzles but with smaller, more complicated pieces and more of them. He will not enjoy playthings that are too complicated for him or toys and games that have no interest for him. But even when children are able to play with more difficult games and puzzles, they usually like to do the old, familiar, simple ones over and over again.

Jeremy, who became so bored with my singing that he made a rude noise, had just recovered from an eye operation. It was important for him to practice eye-hand coordination. Any of the games or puzzles above would have helped him, but he showed no interest in any of them. Even when I took his hand in mine to help him put the blocks in the right places, he was quite bored and uninterested. No amount of encouragement seemed to help, because he had one passion in his life and that passion was cars: cars, trucks, tiny ones, big ones, real or play ones—anything on wheels. He could spend hours playing on the floor with them or staring at them going by on the road outside.

Every day we tried to get him to try one of the games or puzzles on the table, but he could hardly wait to get away to his beloved cars. Then one day he noticed a new jigsaw puzzle. He grabbed it immediately and began putting it together all on his own. It was incredible. Then we saw that the jigsaw puzzle he had chosen had a car in it!

There are many other activities which encourage children to use their hands. Clay is a great favorite, either the kind you buy or the homemade variety. It is a good idea to provide a proper place such as a play table or kitchen table and also set aside a little time to show your child some of the different things he can do with clay. Do not spend too much effort on creating recognizable objects—remember, your goal is to have him learn to use his hands. Show him how to pat, roll, bang, poke, squeeze, tear, pick, and press. Do these things with gusto, show him that *this* is the enjoyment of playing with clay. He has to be able to do all these things *before* he can actually create something. As he learns what he can do with the clay, he will discover for himself how to make snakes and eggs, balls and worms, plates and doughnuts, and so on. The important thing is not what he makes with the clay but how he plays with it.

The same idea applies to finger paints. The important thing is for the child to enjoy seeing what happens as he smears the paint over the table, making patterns with his fingers and then erasing them with a sweep of his hand, only to discover that he has made yet another design. (Finger paints work better directly on a flat surface, such as a kitchen table, rather than on paper, which can become crumpled up; and it is easier to clean up afterward with a wet sponge.) Do not expect your child to be particularly interested in the designs he makes; at this point he is more interested in discovering the possibilities, in learning to use the tools for creativity—his own hands and eyes.

Besides finger paints and clay, other materials which a child handles directly with his hands and fingers are water and sand. In his bath or at the sink, in a sandbox or at the beach he discovers more about what his hands can and cannot do—how dry sand trickles through his fingers, how to cup his hands to get a drink, how to splash, and how to dig holes. The beach on a warm summer day is the ideal playground.

Children are seldom busier—or learning more—than when playing at the water's edge.

Paper is another favorite plaything for children, though adults are sometimes dismayed when a child is so much more interested in playing with the wrapping paper than with the gift inside it. Tearing, ripping, crumpling, folding, and creasing paper show the child even more things he can do with his hands.

Unlike other living creatures, human beings use tools and utensils which enable them to do many things better, quicker, and more efficiently. Thus writing with a pen or pencil is obviously better than dipping a finger in paint. Eating sandwiches by hand is one thing, but soup requires the use of a spoon. If you want to take water from one place to another you need a cup or a bowl or a pail.

From a very early age, children have to be able to use these everyday tools and utensils and it takes practice before they can use them skillfully.

Learning to drink from a cup and eat with a spoon and fork takes time. In the same way, painting with a brush, coloring with crayons, marking with pens and pencils, cutting with scissors take time and practice. This practice can be an enjoyable learning experience—in other words it can be *play* for the child.

All too often, adults impress upon a child the idea that he must produce some finished product from this kind of play. They expect a picture, for instance, and what is more, they expect it to *be* something—they even ask, "What is it?" or suggest to the child what it might be: "Is it a monster?" For the child, all he is doing is making marks on paper with his pencil, paintbrush or crayon. He is not *making* anything, not even a picture. He is simply in the process of discovering what he can *do* with pencils and paints and crayons and paper. He needs this kind of play because this is the way he learns how to use these basic creative tools.

At this early stage the child needs plenty of paper—good sized sheets and not too flimsy. At first he may find broad-tipped felt pens easier to use than crayons. Crayons have to be pressed

quite hard to make a satisfactory mark, and he may not be able to do this right away. Poster paints (nontoxic of course) are the best for children. To begin with, give the child only one color and a short-handled, one-half to one-inch brush. Later on he can experiment with more than one color and can see what happens when he mixes them together—red and blue, blue and yellow, yellow and red—or adds a touch of white to any of these primary colors. One of the joys of parenthood is watching your child's reaction the very first time he paints with a brush or mixes different colors together.

A little girl called Barbie was fascinated when she saw me painting beside her, so I put the brush in her hand, but she would not move her arm. Instead she just held onto the brush and stared at it. I took hold of her wrist and moved it so that she was painting on the paper. She was delighted with the result, but when I removed my hand from her wrist, she stopped painting right away. Then she reached over with her free arm for my hand which she then placed on her wrist again. It took her quite a few moments to realize that she did not need me to guide her wrist in order for her to paint!

It takes time to discover how to handle a paintbrush, a pen, or a crayon, so do not expect your child to be able to pick up a pair of scissors and know how to use them right away. You will probably have to show him where to put his fingers and then hold your hand over his until he starts to use the correct cutting motion. When you buy scissors for your child to use, try them out to be sure they work easily. Sometimes the cheap ones simply do not cut very well, or they are stiff and hard to manage. And, of course, the scissors should have blunt ends.

By this time you will notice whether your child prefers his right or his left hand. As he uses spoons, brushes, crayons, and pencils you will find that he tends to use one hand much more than the other. Encourage him to use *this* hand—the one that he prefers. Do not try to change his handedness. It may look awkward to you if you are right-handed and your child is a southpaw or vice versa, but this tendency has probably been a part of his life ever since he was a baby and first put out his hand to grope for something he could not quite reach.

Right- or left-handedness is not just a question of using one hand or the other. It is more likely to involve the whole side of the body. A left-handed person is very likely left-footed also, and he may rely more on his left eye and left ear as well. So if your child uses his left hand to eat with, he probably kicks a ball with his left foot and leads off with his left foot walking upstairs. Trying to change his handedness will upset and confuse him.

Playing with a variety of things gives children a variety of experiences. The value of these experiences depends on the ability of the child to make use of these playthings. Therefore playthings should be chosen with care. They are as necessary to the preschool child as books are to students. Unfortunately many people think of toys and playthings in the same way that they think of candy—as a special treat, an extra, a very nice but unnecessary addition to the child's regular diet. Actually playthings are essential ingredients for physical and intellectual development and growth in childhood.

Children do not have to have a lot of expensive toys and games, but they do have to have a variety of things to play with. Almost anything will do, provided the child's interests, his likes and dislikes, his ability, and his needs are taken into consideration.

Some of the most successful playthings can be found around the house. An empty cardboard box, big enough to crawl inside, provides endless enjoyment for the toddler. Empty cereal boxes or food cartons taped shut make different-shaped building blocks. Plastic ice-cream containers or round oatmeal boxes or old saucepans become drums to bang with a wooden spoon. Plastic jars with screw tops and a small object inside become rattles. Empty tin cans (make sure there are no sharp edges) of different sizes can be nested inside one another. Mail-order catalogues and old magazines give the child an endless variety of paper to cut or tear or even just to look at. Old blankets can be cuddled. Real dogs or cats that are good with children provide perhaps the best play experiences of all.

When the time comes to buy your child playthings, it is a good idea to think about those things that cannot be duplicated at home. All the endless variety of balls, for instance—little bright-red rubber balls to be grasped in a tiny hand; balloons to be pulled along on a string; big, colorful balls to be kicked and chased after; huge beachballs to roll on; suspended punchballs to be hit over and over again.

Toys on wheels are another category of playthings which cannot be easily made at home: toy cars to be pushed on the floor, or pulled along on a string; wooden wagons big enough to be pushed by the toddler taking his first few tentative steps; wheeled horses and trains on which a child can sit and propel himself along; tricycles he learns to pedal; baby buggies to take out on walks, either play ones with dolls in them or real ones for his baby brother or sister.

Play has rightly been called the work of childhood. It is as important and serious for the child as work is for the adult. But it is also enjoyable and delightful for the child. It is too bad that this enjoyment—this fun—disappears in later life; for so many, the work of adulthood is no fun at all. However we can make certain of our enjoyment of parenthood by sharing our child's delight in *his* work—his work of child's play.

7. a pleasant
personality
is a plus

From the very beginning of life a child responds and reacts to situations, people, and objects. Every child responds and reacts slightly differently from every other child. These differences give a child his own distinct, individual personality. All children, no matter how much slower than average they are, have separate, distinctive personalities. Even those children who look somewhat alike, such as those with Down's Syndrome, have unique, individual personalities. Slower-than-average children have only one thing in common, and that is that all of them behave in a way that would be more appropriate in children who are younger than they are. Otherwise, slower-than-average children are as different from one another as are any other children. Some are outgoing, some are shy, some are excitable, some are timid, some are placid, some are nervous, some are even-tempered, some are aggressive, some are affectionate, some are impatient, some are sensitive, some are cheerful, some are mischievous, some are obstinate, some are withdrawn, some are friendly, some are . . . But the list could go on forever!

All these traits, added together, make up a child's total personality. Personality, to some extent, is something a person is born with, and it is a mixture of behavior traits handed down by fathers and mothers, uncles and aunts, grandparents and great-grandparents stretching back into the past. Everyone is born with a touch of Uncle Fred's laughter, a drop of Great-Aunt Lucy's meanness, and a dollop of Grandpa's temper—and it often comes as something of a shock to recognize an aspect of our own behavior mirrored in our tiny offspring.

However, personality can be altered by circumstances, changed by attitudes, tempered by situations—particularly in early childhood. Things that happen to a child, the way he is treated by others in the first few years of life, influence and shape him. As time goes on and he grows older, he will become less pliable and his personality will be more difficult to change. In other words, it is easier to alter a child's behavior when he is very young than it will be later on when he becomes more set in his ways.

It is important to try to change your child's bad behavior early in life so that his total personality will be as pleasant as possible. An attractive personality is perhaps the greatest gift that parents can give their slower-than-average child. Being accepted and liked by others depends far more on a pleasant personality than on intellectual ability.

However, it is even better to prevent bad behavior from occurring in the first place. One way to do this is to recognize the kind of behavior that can turn into a bad habit later on.

Years ago I knew a little boy named Tom. He had just started walking on his own, and quite by accident he discovered the excitement of being chased. His mother and his older brothers and sisters all thought it was cute the way he would look at them with a mischievous grin on his face and walk off as fast as he could in the opposite direction! Everyone thought it was a great joke to chase after him, and it *was* fun when he was tiny and could not run very fast. But when he grew bigger and could run faster it was not a joke at all. He would slip off and run out into the street before anyone noticed him. Poor Tom could not understand why his family no longer laughed when they chased him, because he still thought it was a very amusing game. And his family did not know how they could break him of this bad habit. Obviously it would have been better if they had not started the game in the first place. Now they had to find a way of stopping him from running away.

It is very difficult for parents to know what to do about this kind of behavior. As a start, divide bad behavior into categories. The first category is so-called dangerous behavior, the next is behavior resulting from carelessness or ignorance, and the last is just plain naughtiness.

Dangerous behavior is the kind of thing that has to be stopped immediately because it can result in real bodily injury or even death. Obviously you are not going to think twice if your child plays with a loaded gun or picks up a bottle of poison. Running away, leaning out of windows, playing with the knobs on the stove or the gears in a car, biting other children, throwing stones, and so forth are all things that have to be stopped immediately—no questions asked, no explanations necessary. There are two or three things you have to do all at once. First you have to physically stop or prevent the child from what he is doing. As you do this you should say "Stop" or "No" in the tone of voice which tells the child you *really* mean it. At the same time give him one sharp, quick slap if you feel it is necessary.

The results of ignorance or carelessness are far more likely to make you angry and want to lose your temper. The following are some common examples of things a child does because he does not know any better: spilling his milk on the floor, emptying the flour bin all over himself, opening the refrigerator and helping himself to an apple, playing with the water in the toilet, scrambling down the basement steps all on his own, and dropping and breaking your favorite ornament.

We should not punish a child for careless behavior, such as dropping or spilling things, any more than we punish ourselves for accidents. However, as much as possible, the child should be encouraged to help clean up afterward.

Playing with water in the toilet may be a favorite pastime for your child, and probably the only way to prevent it is to encourage him to play in the bathtub or at the kitchen sink instead. Make it a fairly regular activity at a time when you can keep an eye on him.

A child can sometimes be prevented from playing with food in the kitchen if you will set aside a low cupboard there which can be filled with playthings. These can be pie tins, plastic containers, muffin pans—anything you can spare which will be "his" and will keep him occupied while you are preparing meals and so on.

Never discourage a child from climbing stairs or steps. It is far better to teach him gradually how to climb safely, as was explained in the last chapter.

There are two ways to prevent the child from damaging ornaments. Either keep your child out of rooms where you keep such ornaments or remove your precious objects until he has got beyond the careless stage of life. The careless stage of life comes at about the time when the child is beginning to walk and explore his surroundings. Like all other stages in the slower-than-average child, this stage comes later in life and it will probably last longer. So it is better for parents to anticipate things and prevent accidents and carelessness by removing obstacles from the reaching hands and unsteady gait of their exploring toddlers.

The last type of bad behavior is naughtiness, and there are several different ways of dealing with this problem. Naughtiness comes about when your child does something which he knows you do not want him to or when he refuses to do something you *do* want him to do.

This kind of behavior can often be prevented by a simple matter of timing and the kind of civility and politeness you normally use with another adult. It would never occur to you to interrupt a bridge player, for instance, in the middle of a game, a golfer on the tee, a businessman at a meeting, or a teacher in class; and yet every day adults interrupt children who are absorbed in their play. Often the consideration of a few minutes warning—"We have to go in a minute or so"; "Supper will be ready very soon"; "Let's get a book and look at it together before bedtime"—will prevent bad behavior. A little tact, a little time, and a little diplomacy often prevent confrontations and head-on collisions with your child. If you can gradually lead him in the path you want him to go you may be able to avoid battles which end up in tears and temper tantrums.

Sometimes parents encourage their children to be naughty and disobedient without realizing what they are doing. Naughty behavior may be the only way a child can get his parents' attention. If you feel your child is being naughty, ask yourself whether you spend more time scolding him than praising him. He may be naughty because he feels this is the only way to get you to notice him.

When temper tantrums do occur and your child

throws himself on the floor in a rage, walk away if you possibly can, or pick him up and put him in his room and then walk away—but do not try to reason with him. Give him the impression that you are ignoring his behavior.

Temper tantrums can be frightening for parents. The child who is on the floor kicking and screaming, working himself to the point where he is blue in the face and shaking all over, gives the impression that he is having a fit. But a real seizure happens unexpectedly, whereas a child throws a tantrum quite deliberately in order to get his own way.

Paul had a temper tantrum when his mother told him it was time to go home from a birthday party. She did not know what to do. Her friend who was giving the party told her to go outside to her car and start it up. In loud voices they said good-bye to each other and, when the hostess closed the front door with a bang, she turned to Paul and said: "My goodness, what are you doing here? Your mother has left already. I wonder if you will be able to catch her. We'd better get outside and see if we can stop her. Hold my hand—let's run." They ran out the door, the hostess shouting, "Stop! Stop! You've forgotten Paul." By then, Paul was beginning to be a bit worried himself, and by the time he got to his mother's car, he was so relieved she had not left without him he had quite forgotten that he did not want to leave the party in the first place.

If you can divert your child's attention in this way you can often avoid problems of behavior. Instead of saying, "You've got to come home now," ask your child to say good-bye to everyone at the party, to show you how well he can put on his new coat, to help you carry your purse, to hold the door open, to remind you to do up your seatbelt, to tell Daddy about the ice cream and birthday cake, and so on.

Experienced baby-sitters, nursery-school teachers, and grandmothers deal with the problem of separation in this way. They know that a child is likely to be afraid of leaving his mother, so they divert his attention while she slips away and they keep him interested until she returns. Each day after that, with the mother's help, they gradually encourage the child to become more aware of her departure until eventually he is able to go through the whole ceremony of leaving her—the hug, the kiss, the waving good-bye—without becoming upset over it.

Sally had been in nursery school for several months and had just about got to the stage where her mother could give her one quick hug before leaving her in the morning. Then one day, because her mother was sick, her father brought her to school instead. Sally left him and went over to her favorite doll and began playing with it. After chatting with me for a few minutes, Sally's father started for the door, but then he realized he had not said good-bye to Sally. He went over to her, gave her a big hug and a kiss, and then walked to the door waving and blowing kisses. Sally dropped her doll. At this point all she saw was her father going away without her, so she immediately burst into tears. He came back, picked her up and hugged her. She stopped crying, thinking he was going to take her with him. The moment he put her down and tried to leave, she burst into tears again. It was a misunderstanding all around. He hated to leave her crying, but he had no choice. He could only hope that eventually she would calm down and dry her tears. How much better it would have been if he had slipped away while she was absorbed with her doll!

Children cannot be expected to part from their parents right away. It takes time and a step-by-step approach to teach them.

When he first came to nursery school, Roddy did not have a problem parting from his mother because he had not got to the stage of noticing very much what was going on around him. Several months later, however, when nursery school had become a familiar daily routine for him, he suddenly began to object when she dropped him off. What had happened was that Rod had developed more awareness. Now he noticed and realized what was happening when she brought him in the mornings. He even got to the stage of anticipating her leaving and began to whimper and make a fuss the moment they turned into the driveway of the school.

It was time to divert his attention. For the next week or so one of the teachers met the car and gathered Roddy in her arms and rushed him into school while his mother drove away as quickly as possible. Gradually over the next few weeks the teacher spent more time collecting Roddy and chatting with his mother before she left. In a step-by-step way Roddy was getting used to the idea of his mother's departure, and eventually he was able to watch her go and even wave her good-bye as she went away.

Another little boy, called Huey, was very close to his mother. In fact one of the reasons for his coming to nursery school was that she felt he had become entirely too dependent on her. He actually would not go to sleep at night unless she lay down beside him! It was going to take more than diversion to persuade Huey that he could manage very well without her. The situation called for some planning.

The first day Huey came to school, his mother stayed with him and took part in all the activities that he did. The second day she stayed in the room with him, but this time instead of joining in she stayed in a corner reading a book. The third day she brought him to school, she stayed in the building but not in the room where Huey was. The fourth day she brought him to school, she left him on his own.

I am not going to try to make you believe that all this was accomplished without tears. As a matter of fact, Huey was so angry with his mother for reading a book that he grabbed it away from her and shoved it in a drawer! And the day she left him entirely on his own he cried for a good twenty minutes. But each day after that his teary spell grew shorter and shorter until eventually he completely forgot how upset he had previously gotten about leaving her.

In situations like these it is no good telling your child that you will be back later on; you have to *show* him. This means he has to experience losing you; he has to learn to deal with your *not* being with him. Obviously you cannot teach him this on your own. You need help from someone else—baby-sitter, grandmother, teacher, or whatever.

A little planning, a step-by-step approach, and some diversionary tactics help to smooth out the rough spots in a child's life. A positive attitude helps too. If you can say firmly, "You're going to have a great time!" instead of "Don't cry, I'll be back to get you right away," you will reassure yourself as well as your child. Remember, *you* know better than he does what is best for him and so you can keep a step ahead of him all the way.

You can keep a step ahead right from the start. One of the first games a child plays is pushing toys out of the crib or off the table and onto the floor. Instead of scolding, parents can make this game a little more complicated by getting the child to throw the toys into a big box. Later on, it is far better to suggest a new game called "Putting toys in the closet," than to say, "Now you'll have to pick them all up again," thus giving him the idea that picking up is not much fun. You may have to help him at first to show him what you want him to do, but if you do it with enthusiasm and enjoyment, then he will probably enjoy doing it too.

If children learn right from the start to tidy up and put things away—"a place for everything, and everything in its place"—then it becomes a way of life rather than an unpleasant chore.

Whenever possible, try to put things to your child in a positive way. Show him what you want him to do and praise him when he does well, rather than constantly drawing attention to him when he has done something wrong. Try to avoid saying over and over: "Don't do that" or "Leave me alone" or "Be careful" or "Hurry up."

As a parent you may feel that all this effort takes an enormous amount of time and patience on your part, but think of it not simply as a way of getting your child to put his toys away, or to get along without you, or even to leave a birthday party without tears, but as a means of teaching him how to deal with new experiences and helping him set up patterns of desirable behavior.

This is what raising a child is all about. In the early years get your child into the habit of greeting you affectionately, of eating with pleasure, of saying "please" and "thank you" and "I'm sorry" at appropriate times, of going to the bathroom, of attempting new activities with enthusiasm, of putting things away where they belong, and of meeting new situations with interest. The child who gets in the habit of behaving acceptably, affectionately, and with consideration for others develops a pleasant personality.

For some reason or other, children take much longer to learn good habits like these than to pick up bad ones. George's first two-syllable word was "Stoopid" and my own daughter's was "Dammit!" and of course there was Dennis' rude noise. Perhaps we encourage bad habits by drawing attention to them. It is well worth a try to give as much attention to your child when he is doing something desirable and to try to ignore his bad behavior—though I must say it is hard to pretend to be deaf when your small child, like mine, repeats a rude word at the top of her voice for all the neighborhood to hear!

The more you notice and praise your child who is doing something well and behaving acceptably the more he will try to please you in this way. Your approval is his reward. What is your reward? Parents of slower-than-average children often feel so disappointed that their child has a low IQ that

they sometimes miss the rewards that all children bring with them into this life.

I'm only going to mention one of them. Children look at the world quite differently from us—they see it in a different light. They see everything for the first time and make discoveries about the world as if they were explorers on an unknown planet. To be a parent is to be given the opportunity to see this unknown planet through their eyes, to look at our own world once again with all the clarity and innocence of childhood.

Slower-than-average children bring us something else as well—something we cannot get from an average child. It is not exactly a reward, but it certainly is a compensation. They give us a chance actually to see how development takes place. In average children events in the early years come about so rapidly, changes take place so quickly, that they cannot be properly observed. The slowed-down pace in our children makes it possible for us to see it happening, so that we can prepare for it, plan for it, and help it to come about. As though watching a slow-motion camera or instant replay on television, we can look at and learn from our slower-than-average child. As we watch the changes slowly unfolding in his life we are learning not only how we can help him but also how to help all other children as well.

Just as Jeff and Billy and Doug showed me how I could become a more effective teacher, so your slower-than-average child gives you the opportunity to be a more understanding parent.

developmental progression

GROSS MOTOR	FINE MOTOR	COMMUNICATION
Head sags	Hands fisted	Throaty noises
Rolls from side to back	Clenches on contact, no release	Single vowel sounds
Prone, lifts head to midline in line with body	Holds object briefly when placed in hand	Eye contact
Supine, vigorous head movements	Glances at toy when placed in hand	Smiles when talked to
Props on forearms, knees flexed, back rounded	Reaches for objects	Laughs, squeals
Rolls over from stomach to back	Grasps objects placed in hand with whole hand	Makes responsive sounds
Balances head	Takes objects to mouth	Coos, chuckles, gurgles, and laughs
Head and chest up 90° when lying on stomach	Plays with fingers	Recognizes mother
Lifts head and shoulders when on back	Eyes follow slowly moving object well	Recognizes human voice
Reaches arms to be pulled to sitting	Looks after toy dropped in sight	Turns head to sound
Rolls over back to stomach	Holds small toys	Smiles when one approaches
Sits alone, back straight; may topple	Bangs and shakes rattle	Smiles at self in mirror
Raises self on extended arms and hands	Plays peekaboo	Listens to his own voice
On stomach can change to sitting position	Transfers objects from one hand to another	"Ma-ma" sounds
Creeps and crawls on all fours	Bangs objects together	Vowel sounds in series
Requires support to walk	Can secure toy by string if string contacted by hand	Knows stranger from family but not afraid
Sits indefinitely	Looks for fallen toy	Deep sounds, grunts
Pulls to standing	Pokes with index finger	Single consonant sounds
Stands by turning first to prone	Uses pincer movement with thumb and forefinger	Tongue play
Walks—wide base, arms flexed	Takes object out of box	Responds to name, "no-no," "bye-bye"
Creeps upstairs	Reaches for image of toy in mirror	Combines syllables
Can go from standing to sitting	Grasps with precision	Copies sounds
Walks well—rarely falls	Cooperates in dressing, raises leg for pants or arm for sleeve	Shows fear of strangers
Climbs into large chairs	Begins to use spoon	1-2 word vocabulary
Walks upstairs with help	Holds cup, tilts cup rather than head causing spills	"Mama" and "Daddy" with meaning
Creeps down steps	Rolls or throws a ball	Waves bye-bye
Seats self in small chair	Builds tower of 2 cubes	Understands very simple commands
Walks, runs, climbs	Scribbles with crayon	Imitates words
Up and down stairs—both feet on one step at a time	Gives up object if hand is held for it	Communicates by gesture
Kicks, squats, jumps	Grasps two objects in one hand	Sensitive to separation from mother
Goes up and down stairs in adult manner	Turns several pages of book at a time	Enjoys looking at picture book
Jumps from bottom step	Builds tower of 3-4 cubes	Points to familiar objects as named by adult
		May carry out two directives
		Vocabulary of 8-10 words
		May combine 2-3 words to express ideas
		Runs simple errands from one room to another

Adapted from "Development According to Mental Age" in *A Helpful Guide in the Training of a Mentally Retarded Child*, Virginia State Department of Health, 1971.

(Gross Motor—continued)

Rides tricycle
Swings and climbs
Balances on one foot
Kicks ball
Walks balance beam
Performs stunts

(Fine Motor—continued)

Removes hat, shoes, socks
Tries to put on shoes
Eats with spoon—spills
Holds glass with two hands
Scribbles with pencil or crayon, vertical strokes
Pulls, carries
Push-pull large toys
Turns door knob
Helps to dress and undress
Tries to button, zips and unzips
Tries to brush teeth
Holds glass with one hand
Uses fork
Uses scissors to chop paper
Builds tower of ten cubes

(Communication—continued)

Uses a few adjectives, prepositions, and pronouns, usually "me" or "mine"
Points to body parts
Uses pronoun "I"
Asks questions
Understands verbal reasoning
Knows sex and name
"Naughty" words
Speech easily understood by outsiders
Counts 1-10
Knows a few colors
Counts three objects
Vocabulary 1,500 words

additional resources

Berieter, Carl and Engelmann, Seigfried. *Teaching Disadvantaged Children in Preschool.* New Jersey: Prentice-Hall, 1966.

Bland, Jane Cooper. *Art of the Young Child.* New York: Museum of Modern Art, 1968.

Bruner, Jerome S. *Toward a Theory of Instruction.* Cambridge: Harvard University Press, 1966.

———. "Child's Play: Developmental Psychology Forum," *New Scientist,* April 18, 1974.

Crelin, Edmund S. *Functional Anatomy of the Newborn.* New Haven: Yale University Press, 1973.

Delacato, Carl H. *A New Start for the Child with Reading Problems.* New York: David Mckay Company, 1970.

Gessell, Arnold; Halverson, Henry M.; and Ilg, Frances L. *The First Five Years of Life.* New York: Harper, 1940.

Haring, Norris, and Schiefelbusch, Richard L., eds. *Methods in Special Education.* New York: McGraw-Hill, 1967.

Lévy, Janine. *The Baby Exercise Book.* Trans. Eira Gleasure. New York: Random House, 1973.

Marzollo, Jean, and Lloyd, Janice. *Learning Through Play.* New York: Harper, 1972.

Mather, June. *Make the Most of Your Baby.* Arlington, Texas: National Association for Retarded Citizens (NARC), 1974.

Perceptual-Motor Foundations: A Multi-disciplinary Concern, Proceedings of the perceptual-motor symposium. Washington, D.C.: American Association for Health, Physical Education and Recreation, 1969.

Radler, D. H., and Kephart, Newell C. *Success Through Play.* New York: Harper, 1960.